A World According

A World According to Women

AN END TO THINKING

JANE McLOUGHLIN

QUARTET

First published in 2009 by
Quartet Books Limited
A member of the Namara Group
27 Goodge Street, London W1T 2LD

A catalogue record for this book
is available from the British Library

ISBN   978 0 7043 7162 0

Typeset by Antony Gray
Printed and bound in Great Britain by
T J International Ltd, Padstow, Cornwall

1

When future students come to review the history of late-twentieth-century Britain, without question the defining feature of the period will be the emergence of women as the dominant factor in shaping our society.

The historians will have the benefit of hindsight, and what will surely puzzle them is the apparent lack of awareness among today's women of what has happened to them. From the 1960s until at least the 1990s the female sex was divided against itself, something we seem scarcely to have noticed. And after the 1990s, the women who set the political, economic and social agenda were not the militant feminists, but the mass of ordinary women who were not even aware that they were taking part in a struggle for domination.

Looking back, it is as though the bulk of the female population sleepwalked into a position of power without recognising what that involved, or the responsibilities it brought. Nevertheless, this apparently whimsical power base is the foundation of the way Britain is being governed today.

In Europe at least, Britain is unique in having a high proportion of the public's power and influence vested in the least politically and economically sophisticated section of the population – so-called 'ordinary' women. These are the housewives and mothers and daughters who keep the domestic economy going. Without such women, society would fall apart. That society seems to be falling apart anyway is down to the inadequacy of the newly feminised system as a basis for power. And that inadequacy is down to the nature of the popular culture which gave these women access to power.

In 1990, the European Union published a research study in which Dr Christine de Panafieu, then working for INSEAD, showed that social advance depended on vital individual 'change-agent' women. Dr de Panafieu quoted 30 per cent as the crucial proportion of change-agent women necessary in the population if there was to be real social advance. Britain, alone in the EU, produced nowhere near that number – just 16 per cent of women met the criteria.

And yet it is in Britain that the women who thus failed so signally to become change-agents have, through a passive, apparently almost semi-conscious, process of infiltration, brought about fundamental social change. Change is not, of course, at all the same thing as progress. Probably few would disagree with the contention that the social change brought about by the empowerment of these women has not really brought greater enlightenment to anyone. It has, though, hugely improved the quality of life for millions of women without their having to make any conscious effort to achieve it. That is down to the nature of their empowerment.

What did empower them?

What happened to unite and empower that vast majority of apathetic housewives and mothers and daughters so that they finally emerged to call the political and economic tune? And why weren't they aware of this great indoor revolution while it was happening?

Popular culture happened, that's what; and the time was right so that en masse ordinary women embraced it. Popular culture was, and still is, the agent of the process of change for the vast majority of women. The reason for the enormous insidious power it has to alter women's values and attitudes lies in its ability to communicate on an almost subliminal level with a mass of people, particularly women. Feminism never achieved anything like this because in general the Women's Movement tried to target women by engaging their brains in intellectual argument. At the time this was the established (masculine) route to understanding. But the new popular culture worked differently; it was easy to understand. Often it aspired to a universal state of childishness, from its use of baby talk and diminutives to the mumsy condescension of magazine-style current affairs programmes like BBC's *Breakfast* or ITV's *GMTV* where the presenters talk to viewers and guests alike in exactly the tone people use to strangers' children. In short, popular culture created a new 'feminine' line of communication, absorbed like a mind-changing drug through women's feelings.

Even if you accept this hypothesis, you are bound to question how this process could happen unless some kind of mastermind with an overriding agenda were pressing the buttons behind the scenes, a form of god-figure organising the creation of a new female life construct. Surely such a mass shift of consciousness could not simply happen?

There was a constant which pervaded all popular culture and always has, always will. It wasn't men; it was money. Every pop culture outlet assumes a reader/viewer and in the interests of profit it had to slant its appeal to groups – particularly women.

This slant guided the first faltering steps of what became

popular culture. Take the start of the career of Jeanne Heal, later the doyenne of women in television.

Jeanne Heal was writing advertising copy for a London agency when the Second World War broke out. She joined the Land Army, stationed in Gloucestershire. At weekends, she hitchhiked to London to keep her hand in at the advertising agency. She wrote to the BBC suggesting a radio talk show about her experiences on the road and the people she met. The BBC commissioned a one-off broadcast. This was heard by a Ministry of Labour official who contacted the BBC to suggest that this girl could do a great morale-boosting job by talking on the radio about life in all the women's wartime services. A celebrity was born!

Money may have been a strong factor in its development, but in the main the motivation of popular culture seems to have happened by accident, the result of a sequence of unplanned and random events a little like the Big Bang theory of how life started on Earth.

True, in the early days, men were in charge of the tools of popular culture's embryonic trade. And men's decisions have played a part in both the development and the fine-tuning of popular culture. But it was always a pragmatic process. Men didn't know what they were doing in this new area of women's interests. They could only react to some perceived female need or demand which would make money. Popular culture reacted to what women wanted, not what men wanted to give them. And it was never averse to a spicing of helpful propaganda to reflect women's growing importance as an audience. Some may like to think of what happened as a male plot, another example of masculine manipulation of women. But would men (even if capable of planning something so cataclysmic) have deliberately set in motion a process which has practically destroyed the grounds of their own then-cherished masculine identity?

Historians studying civil wars use a set of criteria they call the Collier-Hoeffler model, to set out what constitutes a civil war. Judged by those criteria, the divisions between women in the second half of the twentieth century come close to the definition, at least philosophically if not in the degree of violence the protagonists resort to. It seems that the root causes of civil conflict can be reduced to either greed or grievance: that is, the rift within the population is caused either for reasons of identity – ethnicity, social affiliation, religion, and (why not?) gender – or it's in the economic best interests of those who oppose them. The first seems a fairly accurate description of the feminists. The massed ranks of ordinary women were the opposition, traditional women who resisted revolution but were taught by popular culture to see advantage in pursuing their own feminine interests.

Collier-Hoeffler also points out, significantly, that there's an increased risk of civil war with a rise in population. Feminism and popular culture bloomed as the numbers of young adults surged after the baby boom following the Second World War.

Perhaps it is merely whimsical to talk of the struggle between feminists and the rest in such overtly hostile terms. But even so, the way popular culture has developed since the 1960s has allowed ordinary women to emasculate the aggressive efforts of active feminists to raise their consciousness or liberate them from the domination of men.

The feminists failed to achieve anything of the sort. Perhaps they mistook their enemy. They fought the battle for sex equality as a struggle against the tyranny of men and their long-established masculine hierarchical systems. But we're beginning to see now that men were peripheral to the argument. True, men had created the hierarchical systems which determined how women lived and operated. But with women's collusion. Many women, as well as men, saw men's dominant status as pre-ordained in the Garden of Eden. But the rigidity of these masculine systems was crumbling anyway. Actually, if they'd only known it, the feminists' enemy was the mass of ordinary women they couldn't reach with their subversive arguments. The Women's Movement never seemed to realise that the mass of the female population collaborated with the men the feminists saw as their oppressors. Most women didn't particularly want to change the system; they accepted it, as had their mothers and their grandmothers.

By accepting the traditional masculine hierarchies, ordinary women were part of men's defence against the feminists' attacks. And until popular culture opened their eyes to new horizons, most women never questioned this. Even when they did see that they could be leading more rewarding lives, they had no thought of restructuring the masculine system to achieve this.

Popular culture enabled these women to explore and develop their own femininity independently of the dominant male. It gave them for the first time the confidence to trust their female-ness for its own sake because it was not a personal weakness, but common to the mass of women and therefore a source of strength. Unlike the feminists, they did not want to change their essential womanhood. Popular culture gave them a chance to be female and not see this as a disadvantage within a masculine system.

Today popular culture has changed the acquiescence that made them accept the assumption that maleness was essentially superior to the female, which is what women did. Women are now using and developing the source of their empowerment, this femininity, to bring about political and social change in their own interests. The old traditional 'masculine' systems and hierarchies have been almost entirely subsumed in a new 'feminine' political agenda which already prevails throughout society and is enshrined in law. Women's new agenda has imposed new feminine-orientated criteria about what is important in society as a whole, and it is to the popular culture which empowered them that they refer in calling the tune. It seems now that everything that happens is a media event, and that's what matters: more than that, if something is not a media event, it doesn't matter whether it happened or not.

The consequences of this mindset for the world outside popular culture are way beyond the scope of any soap opera scriptwriter or popular songwriter to control. What follows is certainly a horror story, but at least, if we understand what has happened, perhaps, in the best traditions of popular culture, there will be a chance to contrive a happy ending.

2

Popular culture emerged in the late 1960s as the change-agent force it became for women. The time was right, and so was the technology. We have all seen archive film of the coronation of Queen Elizabeth II in 1953, showing the residents of entire terraced streets crammed into the front room of the one house on the block which boasted a television set to watch the ceremony as it happened. Some commentators even mentioned at the time that this marked a new departure, a window on the world available in any humble cottage or suburban semi.

The televising of the coronation actually caused sales of TV sets to rocket. In Parliament, though, Members were divided about allowing television cameras access to the ceremony. They felt that the solemnity of a state occasion would be diminished if the public were to be included, even at a distance. The traditional social order could be destabilised if the people were not kept in their place! Premonitions, perhaps, of the way popular culture might affect political thinking in years to come. It was the Queen herself who made the decision to go ahead. She told the doubters – the Earl Marshal, the Archbishop of Canterbury and Sir Winston Churchill among them – that nothing must stand between the crowning and her people's right to participate.

After that, nothing would hold back the advance of popular culture. By the Sixties, access to television and the radio was growing fast; new mass-market women's magazines were being launched; and an ever wider range of novels were appearing in cheap paperback editions. Ordinary women increasingly had access to the pleasures and diversions of popular culture in their own traditional territory, their family living rooms.

This was important because at that time it was still difficult for a woman to go out on her own to restaurants, pubs or even the cinema. Which is as much as to say, she had no access to an independent social life or entertainment except when accompanied by a man. A woman friend remembers as late as the 1970s how she and her fiancé were working on the *Newcastle Journal,* and she waited for him in the taxi line at Central Station for four hours while he went to the farewell party of a colleague – a colleague of them both, incidentally – held in a men-only pub. And another journalist friend was asked to leave the top Manchester hotel where she was staying on business when she went into the bar alone for a drink. If she wanted to drink, she could do so in her room. She was told, 'We don't want the hotel to get a bad name.'

That sort of attitude illustrates why it was important that women could experience popular culture in their own homes. At least there they were free to explore what interested them without being inhibited by society's blanket assumption that any woman who looked for entertainment or even refreshment outside the home and without the presence of a man must be a whore.

This kind of outrageous prejudice explains why feminism emerged as a would-be mass political movement. The anger and frustration behind the Women's Movement was not intended to be exclusive. It set out to speak for all women and in doing so alarmed and alienated many. Even so, in the big cities particularly, women were becoming a subject for discussion. Simone de Beauvoir had opened her seminal book on women, *The Second Sex*, translated and published in Britain in the Fifties, with this: 'For a long time I have hesitated to write a book on woman. The subject is irritating, especially to women . . . ' But irritating or not, the new British female intelligentsia – women born in the post-war baby boom, the highly educated beneficiaries of the 1944 Education Act, many of them the products of the new red-brick universities or the previously all-male colleges of Oxford and Cambridge – were forcing the issues of their situation into the male arena as a legitimate subject for debate.

This, though, is where the rift opened up within the female sex. The public debate tended to be limited to feminist activists and failed to convince the mass of ordinary women that there was justification for rebellion.

Ordinary women were less aware of the degree of male chauvinism in society because in their day-to-day lives they had less direct confrontation with it than did female careerists working with men outside the home. For women in the domestic setting gender inequality was part of the facts of life. Nor were there easy ways for them to find out what was going on. At this point, the real debate was going on in America, where, by 1961, President Kennedy had already made women's rights a key issue, and established a high-level Presidential Commission on the Status of Women. This side of the Atlantic, there was a feeling that women here were playing catch-up. While British feminists read Betty Friedan's *The Feminine Mystique* and the novels of Erica Jong, the one aspect of the issue that engaged ordinary women in the UK was the tennis match called 'The Battle of the Sexes' when Billie-Jean King beat her male challenger, a former champion, Bobby Riggs. Television made that available for the mass of women to watch as part of popular culture; amazingly it is still the most viewed tennis match in history.

Mood, of course, is contagious, while rational argument is not. Creating mood was how popular culture operated as part of mass communication. It tuned in to basic female dreams and generated states of emotional readiness which amount to moods. As a result, ordinary women became more restless within the confines of the male-orientated system, and more susceptible to the idea of change.

We might as well deal here and now with this phrase 'ordinary women', and get it over with. In itself, of course, it is meaningless. But anyone trying to differentiate between women in terms of a mass market, as opposed to the minority special interest group which the feminists became, must come up against the same inadequacy of language. I use 'ordinary women' to describe the bulk of the female population who are housewives and mothers and daughters, who may well work outside the home, but whose priorities are still primarily home and family. Their jobs are probably fairly mundane, and not highly skilled. Basically these were women who saw their identity as part of a marriage, a family or a community whose interests they would put first if they came into conflict with ambitious self-interest. This would apply, too, to their personal ambitions on a wider stage. By and large, these are women who did not set out to change the world.

At the start of the Sixties, the vast majority of ordinary women had little independent spending power. Men's wages provided for the family. Women budgeted for the household, but it was not their own money, and any money they spent on themselves was at the expense of the family and therefore a source of guilt. To spend on their own pleasure was positively sinful. At least popular culture had the advantage of being comparatively cheap.

Popular culture also needs definition. For the purposes of this book, this is used to mean the prevailing vernacular culture shared at a simple and direct level by the majority of people through fashion, advertising, television, newspapers and magazines, and, of course, music. It is strongly associated with commercial products, and changes constantly as mass taste demands ever new sensations to avoid boredom. Raymond Williams in *Keywords*, published in 1983 by Fontana, defines the word popular in connection with culture in four ways: 'well-liked by many people'; 'inferior kinds of work'; 'work deliberately setting out to find favour with the people'; and 'culture actually made by the people for themselves'. All these interpretations have a part to play in the argument of this book.

But in my view popular culture has an additional factor which gives it the capability – literally a mind-blowing capability – to bypass the rational process of the brain in order to evoke emotion to change mood and therefore affect behaviour. In the late Seventies, Bob Payton, an advertising executive for J. Walter Thompson, expounded the theory that you could sell any product to any woman if you could associate it with the music that had been popular at the most emotionally charged period of her life – when she was first kissed, for instance. The point is, the music – always this was popular music based on sentiment, not music requiring mental effort – is a kind of top-up dose of a moment when emotion and physical pleasure melded. Perhaps Bob Payton's hypothesis – which has proved a highly successful advertising device – was not so different from Noel Coward's 'Extraordinary how potent cheap music is' in *Private Lives*. Popular culture has always adapted its mass messages accordingly, even if its targets are unaware of this subliminal nostalgia.

But to go back to the beginning. The new technological advances gave ordinary women access to television, and to new popular music they could afford within their own homes. These first tastes of popular culture were thus part of the household routine, not to do with a special occasion. Nor did it make demands on them. Unlike traditional culture (which accentuates the divide between the educated and uneducated and tends to exclude mass audiences), popular culture sets up less of a barrier to messages which are absorbed through the senses rather than the mind.

Its impact on women also has to be seen in the light of their situation when they first had mass access to the new media. Many had been brought up in highly structured and disciplined households where husbands and fathers controlled their wives' and daughters' access to information and entertainment in the home – the radio, records, books; and films at the local cinema. Men were usually the ones who decided how the family passed their leisure time, probably limiting the hours which could be 'wasted' on trivial entertainment. Light literature, pop music, fashion statements, were commonly seen as trivial and time-wasting if not actually occasions for sin. Certainly most men didn't go to the lengths of the legendary explorer Charles Doughty, the author of *Arabia Deserta*, who earlier in the century wouldn't allow his two daughters to read fiction at all because novels were all made up and therefore told lies. But nonetheless it was quite common well into the Sixties for the male breadwinner in a household to screen what the family watched on television, listened to on the radio, or the books they read for pleasure. Even today, women still complain that men automatically take possession of the remote control.

But in the early days of mass popular culture, women were becoming frustrated. They could see that society was changing around them, that class barriers were disappearing, and yet none of this had changed their lives for the better. What they had accepted without question before 1939 no longer seemed so immutable after 1945.

Society has never really acknowledged how betrayed millions of women felt in the aftermath of the Second World War. But they would have felt like traitors to say so. Partly, perhaps, that's because most women felt it inappropriate to make a fuss or plead their cause when society as a whole was finding it so hard to return to any kind of normality.

But these women had filled in for the men who were away fighting, in every sense. They had been Land Girls and lorry drivers and they had worked in industrial factories manufacturing weapons and equipment for the war. They had done this in circumstances which may well have kept them in a constant state of physical fear, and certainly ceaselessly worried about those they loved. There was a joke current in Liverpool during the worst of the bombing: 'Where's your husband?' one woman asks another. She replies, 'The coward's at the Front.' Such women had spent the war years living in a terrible present where the future was too confused and frightening to contemplate. But they had to force themselves to believe it would be better than the past. Then, when the men came home and tried to pick up the pieces of their lives and return to normal, they needed, as well as expected, to take back the jobs the women had been doing.

Men took it for granted that women would be content to return to their pre-war status quo at the kitchen sink, breeding for Britain. That was the normality they themselves were trying to recapture and they assumed – if they thought about it at all – that this must be the same for women.

But for ordinary women that status quo was even tougher and more dreary than it had been before the war. The men had invariably been changed by their experience; often they seemed like strangers to their own families. Men's aspirations had been changed by the way the war had broken down barriers between classes, and there was a strong movement towards a more just society at all levels. Women were not required to be active in this movement, they remained passive participants in change.

There was no let-up in the bureaucratic interference such as the rationing which continued long after the war was over. Women could not protest because returning men were taking back the reins as breadwinners and arbiters of family life. These men had been prepared to give their lives to preserve what they had had before the war; now they demanded a better world and they voted Labour to get it. But women were out on a limb; confined once more to home and family, they could do little to change the male hierarchical systems that they now felt curtailed as well as controlled their lives.

This was not a question of blame. Many men were returning from mind-blowing experiences which had forced them to live life more intensely than ever before. What they had seen had traumatised them, but also, for many, it had been the most exciting and invigorating time of their lives. They came home expecting to find a new land fit for heroes to live in, and, of course, it wasn't anything of the kind. They felt alienated from women they could not talk to about what had happened to them. They could, however, go out to the pub or a working men's club to be with men who had shared their experiences. Women were not part of that mutual understanding. Men found it difficult to express their feelings or talk to their wives to reveal their complex state of mind.

Many perfectly ordinary women felt a sense of anti-climax, if not disappointment. This made them feel guilty. They had tasted independence and freedom, and they had enjoyed the unprecedented camaraderie of being part of a team and mixing with other women. They had enjoyed a new sense of fulfilment from working outside the home. But how could women express that to psychologically volatile men who might take what they said to mean that as far as their wives and girlfriends were concerned they might have been happier if they had never returned?

Women put the best face on it they could. The war, a majority thought, had ostensibly been fought to build a better world, and in unprecedented numbers women played their part in that better future by dutifully getting pregnant and trying to settle back into a family life of domestic optimism. Men perceived their wives' willingness to have children as a sign that all was well; far too many of them thought quite sincerely that a baby was all any woman needed to make her happy. It occurred to very few men to try to imagine what their wives might have been through. Nor, in the face of the horrors of war at the sharp end, could women explain what they had endured at home. To say so would have seemed disloyal and ungrateful. Of course it was nonsense to imagine women on the home front being 'protected' from the horrors of war; there was the blitz on all major cities, then the horror of the V1 and V2 rockets.

Women felt guilty at their discontent. They resented men's assumption that women could simply pick up their lives where they had left off because of the war, but they blamed themselves for feeling as they did.

In many ways, though, things were worse for women than they had been in 1939. They were lonely – living with a virtual stranger at home, the camaraderie of war work reduced to post-war hours spent queuing for still-rationed basic necessities. It did not feel like victory. But those queues became an early form of popular cultural exchange, the one place where women could begin to talk to each other. But the argot of the queue was complaint. 'Don't you know there's a peace on?' they'd say. A trouble shared is a trouble halved, was a phrase much used then. Waiting around like that, women could share the negative experiences they were going through. Amongst themselves they did what they could not do in front of men. They complained about their lot. They criticised men in general, taking out their resentment against their husbands because amongst themselves they would not be held to account for it. The women all seemed to be in the same boat.

And they grumbled at the government of a country which, though victorious, kept rationing in place longer than any other European country. Women learned then that they would get no help or support from the politicians who ran the country. It was in the interests of those men in government to ignore women as individuals but to impose on their forbearance as wives and mothers. It was in the government's interest to stereotype every woman as the pivotal heart of the family which must play a crucial role in helping restore men to their former status outside the home as workers and consumers. In other words, men must be cogs keeping the industrial, economic and social structure stable, and women were there to make the machinery work.

Yet the war had proved to the mass of women that they could meet any demands society made on them. But men scarcely noticed; and they were making no concessions. Even a Labour government and post-war socialist dreams of class equality in the Fifties offered ordinary women little to hope for outside the traditional role of wife and mother. Class obsessed the masculine hierarchies, but not women; it was not the issue that involved them. Women have never been defined by class as men were. Many were social climbers and snobs, but they were so much more mobile socially, categorised as they were according to the social and financial standing of their husbands or fathers. Class equality for many women could actually close a major route to improving their social status.

Women worried at how empty their lives felt in spite of the traditional fulfilment of motherhood. The journalist Sally Vincent made a short series of films for the BBC in the Sixties asking ordinary women to talk about their lives. One interviewee expressed, without rancour but as a fact of life, how, on having her first child, she realised that that was all she could hope for out of her life. She had expected a sense of fulfilment, of achievement, and all she felt was that this was 'it'. She'd felt cheated and disappointed. It wasn't what she'd been promised; she had believed her prince would come and then she would live happily ever after. Why hadn't anyone warned her?

In response to that programme, thousands of women wrote to the BBC thanking this woman for putting words to exactly their own feelings. 'I thought I was alone', or 'I felt so guilty, no one ever told me it would be like that', were typical comments. What astonished Sally Vincent was their universal lack of bitterness at the way they saw themselves as having been conned.

It was a fair question, though. Why did women not warn others of what might happen to them, and how they might feel? Well, what was the point? Nothing could change the outcome. The social system needed babies; warning mothers of the impending anti-climax of birth might put them off.

The male-orientated political preoccupations of the time, then, made ordinary women feel more than ever removed from participating in decisions about their own lives. They felt that this was unfair; for the first time, in the war, they had been aware that they could be persons in their own right, not simply functionaries within the family. Yet in practical terms there was nothing they could do to help themselves. But these women were in the right frame of mind to look outside marriage and the family for something or someone who understood their needs.

So when the new media in the Sixties did engage a mass female audience, women began to see they had more in common with each other than they had with the traditional male system. And they had learned from their experience after the war not to trust the men who operated those masculine hierarchies.

This opened up women's potential as a new mass market which the various arms of popular culture were quick to exploit. At first, this popular culture was confined to what was broadcast on the radio or watched on television; it included, too, popular music on records and what was read in mass-circulation newspapers and magazines. The effect of those forms of popular culture impacting on women audiences led to expansion into new, associated, areas like advertising, fashion and, particularly, shopping. Popular culture's scope became broader as its areas of female interest created new consumer demand. And all the while groundbreaking technology offered new cultural sources and scope for choice, reaching its apotheosis with the Internet and the world-wide web.

Early on, popular culture began specifically to target ordinary women. This was particularly so once daytime television started. Women were largely popular culture's 'users'. Men's culture was still based on sport and the pub, both of which took them out of the home. They were not particularly interested in what popular culture offered, whereas for women it became a tool of their domestic trade. It kept the children occupied, and pop music helped housework go with a swing. Women's programmes on radio and TV encouraged them to make the best of themselves to boost their self-esteem. Popular culture gave women something to talk about at the Women's Institute or the Townswomen's Guild or the Mothers' Union, broadening their horizons beyond their immediate community.

We're talking here about a process that works through entertainment and sensual gratification: it provides distraction, not debate; emotional involvement, not rationale; sentimentality, not mental effort. Also, while it is absorbed individually, it is part of the common experience of the mass audience, which creates a kind of emotional bonding on the part of its recipients. There is no intrinsic message or meaning in a work of popular culture. It generates empathy, not ideas.

So this phenomenon, which was beginning to have such a profound and provocative effect on the mass of women, is, by definition, a force without high moral or didactic purpose, nor even a particular intention to provoke thought or ideas.

Yet from the beginning it was enormously powerful. The key to popular culture's revolutionising effect on ordinary women's lives was access. While only two per cent of the UK population went to the theatre, opera, ballet, museums and art galleries, 98% watched 25 or more hours of television a week and 94% listened to the radio. In the safe and familiar environment of women's own homes popular culture brought the outside world to them. They saw how other women lived, and were free to react to what they saw and heard without guilt or inhibition.

Moreover, this new communication tool was tailored to appeal to them; it spoke to them directly, not as household functionaries, but as individuals. No matter if each individual was instantly absorbed into the mass mentality of others just like herself. Each woman felt she was taken seriously as a person, not a cipher, and it was on a personal level that she empathised with Elsie Tanner in *Coronation Street* or Dusty Springfield singing her heart out on record. In their millions these ordinary women felt uplifted as they embraced the world which popular culture opened up to them. It was a world of heightened emotion, of gut feeling; it was cathartic. And they felt happier for it.

Mass culture is powerful because it is popular. It is popular because it satisfies the deep-seated longing for understanding felt by the women it is aimed to seduce.

3

Before we look in more detail at the process which enabled popular culture to communicate and become part of the consciousness of the mass of women at grass-roots level, we have to ask why the feminists failed to gain the sympathy and support of these women.

The Women's Movement was gathering momentum at this point. Women's groups were set up in towns and cities all over the country, mostly comprising married graduate housewives who were bored out of their minds with the sudden brake put on their hopes and interests when they married and had children. They missed having other women to talk to on a rational level, the intense sense of discovery and intellectual excitement of university, and the freedom to explore their own potential. It was intoxicating, particularly when combined with the new sexual freedom with a wide choice of available young men. Sexual freedom, though, was not unique to universities; it was the intellectual stimulus, where gender was irrelevant, that had a profounder effect on women graduates.

So when they launched themselves on what they had been led to believe was an expectant world of careers, they resented being excluded by aspects of their femininity from the male world of work and political power. These women weren't looking for some kind of emotional apotheosis, they wanted the same intellectual stimulation they saw men taking for granted.

Their initial response was to deny their own femininity

by aping men, leaving a farcical perception of feminists as bra-less lesbians in dungarees with Dr Martens on their feet. They organised themselves in hierarchic groups, including working-class women because at that time male-orientated society was preoccupied with the class struggle. The working classes then were in the political ascendant with a high-profile political case to argue. The feminists took this on board. They noted the growing influence of trades unions based on the amalgamation of the weakest members of the workforce, and so saw power and change as lying with the lowest common denominator in society. If that was the industrial working class, that was the image they set out to project for themselves. Middle-class privilege was anathema to them; women made up a fictional background of deprivation or victimisation for themselves; they abandoned their plum-in-the-mouth accents and learned to talk like truckers; they eschewed their chinless-wonder peer group dates to sleep with bits of rough they thought would give them working-class credentials.

It was absurd, of course, but it was all great fun for them. None of it, though, impinged directly on the daily lives of the vast majority of ordinary women. Only some six per cent of women at that time went to university. Even so, women were becoming a political issue. The newspapers were full of the activities of the 'Women's Libbers'. Women were achieving legal and political advances like the introduction of the contraceptive pill for unmarried women, and, in 1968, legalised abortion. Popular culture was reflecting these new areas for emotional conflict to exploit in the highly charged storylines of TV soaps and in the problem pages of the newspapers and magazines.

This is not intended to belittle those early feminist

activists and what they achieved on the legal and political front. It's worth noting that in Ulster where, because they were involved in a different kind of struggle, women activists were less focused specifically on women's rights, and the Abortion Act, for example, has still not been extended to the province. This might suggest that the aggressive canvassing of the Women's Movement was a definite factor in bringing about such progress.

The feminists did also succeed in achieving legislation to further women's rights with the 1970 Equal Pay Act and the 1975 Sex Discrimination Act, both crucial to improving women's rights in society.

The mass of women, though, saw these changes simply as an aspect of the predominant masculine hierarchical system of government. They saw them as concessions from men, less as entitlements wrested from them by feminist activists. The mass of women absorbed these legal changes reactively, not as active participants in change. Even with anti-discrimination legislation in place, they rarely tried to push it to their full advantage.

The feminists, though, were at least ensuring that women were becoming part of the political agenda. Women's issues which had been seen as subordinate clauses to central policy arguments became part of mainstream debate. The *Guardian* women's page ran a regular feature called 'Naked Ape' highlighting examples of men's chauvinism. Issues of women's unequal status were discussed in all the 'quality' newspapers and magazines.

The trouble was that once the feminists had secured at least a legal and political framework for gender equality, they did not consolidate the ground they had won. If they had, they might have won the hearts and minds of the unaligned ordinary women. Instead they committed the worst sin in the popular culture code of practice; they became predictable. That lost them the attention of all those women whose empowerment depended on the instant gratification that the mass media provided to satisfy their demands. Frustrated feminists became more strident, demanding positive discrimination in their favour which in many cases the masculine system, rather than men, could not have sustained had they achieved it. The feminists had no alternative administrative set-up in mind, only that more women should be involved in the one that already existed – the male-orientated system which the majority of ordinary women still saw as being where their personal security lay.

So most of them persisted in the view that feminists were outsiders within their own sex. Often it was as though the activists didn't speak the same language. In many ways, they did not recognise each other as full members of the same gender. Ordinary women felt the feminists were repudiating what they considered real womanhood; the feminists were contemptuous of ordinary women because their female aspirations were limited to husband, home, and family, thus colluding in their own servitude.

Perhaps *because* it was aimed at the mass constituency of women, and thus by definition trivial, the feminists never took popular culture seriously as a political rival.

But the feminists misjudged the situation. Access to the seduction techniques of popular culture had broadened the scope of ordinary women's aspirations beyond expectation. Perhaps, because they were idealists, the feminists also underestimated the commercial cynicism of the men who were ultimately in charge of the media, whose motives were profit and increased consumption. These men took advantage of the lack of understanding between the feminists and ordinary women. Confident that they were winning the battle for the hearts and minds of the majority of women, these men were sure enough of their support base to treat the feminist cause as faintly ludicrous. They invited their female audiences to look on the sisters as clowns.

So ordinary women did not get the opportunity to see the feminist message as a serious cause for concern. The mass media combined to make sure that it was never presented as anything but absurd, an argument that could be dangerous if it weren't so ridiculous. All too often when women had their say in the letters columns of the *Daily Mail* or the *Express*, these started off, 'I'm not a Women's Libber but . . . ' The *Sun* and the *Mirror* poured scorn on readers of the *Guardian* women's page – and particularly the 'Queen Ratbags', its feminist writers. In the end too many women seemed to think they had to apologise for criticising the way the masculine world treated them. The result was that the mass of women saw the activists of the Women's Movement in terms of antics rather than genuine protest relevant to themselves. Many opposed them because they did not want to be associated with women they saw as acting outside what was considered feminine.

And for their part the activists were not significantly aware of the effects of popular culture. They seem to have concentrated their efforts on sympathisers, and dismissed those who weren't as beneath contempt. They were always more interested in converting men than they were in convincing ordinary women. For most women, though, men were what they wanted. They liked men. They wanted someone to love them, someone who cared for them, someone they could trust, and for that another woman was a potential rival, not a substitute.

A few feminists tried to combat this disastrous under-estimation of what popular culture was doing to ordinary women. Germaine Greer, then a lecturer at Warwick University, tried to break down the barriers between an academic intelligentsia and the woman in the street by co-starring with comedian Kenny Everett on *Nice Time*, a 1968/9 light-hearted family show from Granada Television, while she was writing the iconic *The Female Eunuch* (1970), but her efforts were perceived as at best tokenism, at worst freakish.

Generally speaking, as Angela McRobbie wrote in *Gender and Generation*, 'academic women tended to underestimate the resources and capacities of ordinary women and girls to participate in their own struggles as women but quite autonomously.'

At the same time, ordinary women were still often isolated from one another on an emotional level. Even if they lived in the same street, they often had a more intimate emotional connection with a character in a soap opera than they did with their neighbours.

Before the explosion of popular culture in the Sixties, Simone de Beauvoir used the Hegelian argument of innate hostility to the 'Other' to explain that male hostility to women is inbuilt, but she went on to say that women, individually Other, had no shared consciousness with the mass of other women. That is the mind-set that Sixties popular culture set out to change.

A few 'ordinary' women did organise political initiatives – for example, the 1968 Dagenham Women sewing machinists' strike at Ford over regrading and pay parity – but they had little relevance for the mass. Most women simply did not understand what the academic and intellectual political feminists were on about. They were afraid of them and their disruptive attitudes. This suspicion was rooted in ordinary women's fear of the unknown, and an unwillingness to cause too much damage to the status quo.

How could they understand them, when the feminist activists marked the male gender down as the enemy? Ordinary women could not participate in a sex war in their own homes and families, where most of them still depended on the support they got from men. The majority of women felt protected by this. They could see no point in rebelling against it.

Those were times of huge political and social upheavals about issues like class and race and extremism. On the whole those questions were more immediate to most women than feminist issues. The radicalised generation of educated young people emerging from the new universities and polytechnics were questioning the values and morality of the establishment, dismissing the conservatism and securities of the past. Youth was on the march – about the nuclear bomb; about the power structure and the role of the state versus the individual. Amongst these young people, women were no longer excluded simply because of their gender from participating in the intellectual excitement of the times.

The mass of women saw all this as a threat, too. In effect, apart from that general turbulence, feminist activists had no effective, specific power base for action of their own except for gender; but in using gender as a weapon, they cut themselves off from the real lives of the mass of women. Political feminists – too often educated middle-class careerists with little connection or contact with ordinary women –

certainly tried to use contemporary culture to proselytise, but theirs was not mass popular culture. They created feminist ghettos which in effect were elitist, not popular – Buzz Goodbody started the Women's Street Theatre Group, and the Women's Theatre Festival; *Spare Rib* and Virago were women-only areas which were seen by the mass of women (if they were aware of them at all) as seeking to divorce them from the central core of their lives – men.

Feminists wanted to infiltrate the political and intellectual power bases which were dominated by men and male interests. We can see with hindsight that their interest in ordinary women was academic, even theoretical, intended to provide a political constituency.

These educated feminists predominately studied arts; on graduation they couldn't get into male-dominated economic and political hierarchies or into government in significant numbers. They went instead into the media.

This did not bring them directly closer to ordinary women. Even the language of feminism drove a wedge between the Women's Movement and ordinary women. Germaine Greer in *The Female Eunuch* wrote brilliantly and clearly, but even so her language seemed academic and erudite. Words are often daunting, as anyone who fills in their own tax return knows well. And the communication gap between women did not get better: picking words at random from pages of feminist treatises today, we meet 'visualities', 'decentring', 'televisual apparatus', 'cyberfeminism', 'medical/scientific construction of fetal personhood' . . . Such words and concepts may be clear to the feminist intelligentsia, but not to most ordinary women. Even the computer spellchecker fails to recognise them.

George Bernard Shaw in *Pygmalion* said that an Englishman can't open his mouth to speak without making another Englishman hate him. The feminists should have taken note. The new popular culture, on the other hand, gave ordinary women the means to communicate with each other without putting each other down. Marshall McLuhan pointed out in *Understanding Media* (1964) how 'the effect of TV was to form a single all-inclusive and instantaneous web of communication that eliminated both hierarchy and distance'.

In the end the feminists failed as a mass movement because they did not engage with ordinary women. They were not interested in what such women wanted because that was exactly what was implicated in the systems they wanted to demolish.

But where the feminists failed, popular culture only too comprehensively triumphed.

4

In the Sixties and Seventies popular culture was showing the mass of women who were not part of feminism a vision of what they could aspire to, and encouraging them to demand it. In effect, on the one hand the media was telling them what they hadn't realised they wanted, and on the other, giving it to them.

For the first time, on TV and the radio, in magazines and in the words of popular records, ordinary women, the mothers of the baby-boomers, could see on television and hear on radio programmes like *Woman's Hour* other ordinary women in very different circumstances to themselves describing and talking about their lives. A suburban housewife chatting about herself and her husband Jim spoke directly on the much-listened-to radio soap, *Mrs Dale's Diary*, to previously oblivious women in terraced streets in Manchester or in a high-rise flat in Gateshead about what her daily life entailed, and those women recognised that they were fundamentally alike. It also made them question their own circumstances and attitudes in a situation which held no fear or threat to themselves. Popular culture, particularly television, had the effect of dispelling women's fears of the unknown, and even of each other, by making the things they were afraid of – loneliness, poverty, losing their man, being unloved and all the other worries and insecurities that come with being a homebound female – appear as part of the domestic norm. They were not alone. Men had work, and children had school, as reference points to connect them to society as a whole. Women were isolated in their own homes and they were profoundly lonely. Even within the Women's Institute or the Townswomen's Guilds or the Mothers' Union or at church, they were identified as wives and mothers. Well into the Eighties, long-standing members still commonly addressed each other as Mrs Smith or Mrs Jones rather than by their Christian names. Such formality is intimidating to friendship or confidences.

Popular culture played out emotional situations women feared. They were used to being jealous of other women – in the basic meaning of jealousy as fear of losing what you thought you possessed – because they saw them as rivals who might deprive them of their husbands. Through popular culture, though, they began to see that they did not have to be afraid of them. They were united by seeing for themselves how much they had in common with others in different places and walks of life, but, ultimately, because as women they were in the same situation. They gained understanding and sympathy for *la condition féminine*. They no longer felt isolated from other women. Popular culture was their new best friend, all the more so because it was new best friend to millions of others.

Perhaps, too, as part of this new broad community of women like themselves, they first felt significant as individuals in the world outside their own homes. They were able to feel that they counted within a new female solidarity in the wider world similar to that to which their husbands and children already had access through work and school. For the first time they felt that they had a degree of power about the way they experienced their own lives. In effect, popular culture fostered a real sisterhood because it was all about what women had in common.

They could begin to trust each other because of what popular culture told them they shared – their feelings, desires, ambitions and values – however different their circumstances.

George Orwell wrote in the mid-1940s, 'The average man is not directly interested in politics and when he reads he wants the current struggles of the world to be translated into a simple story about individuals. People worship power in the form in which they are able to understand it.'

If he had said the same thing in 1970, he would probably have specified women, not men.

For ordinary women, this embryonic sense of empowerment did not involve society outside their own community of popular culture. Ordinary women's view of themselves and their role was changing in reaction to the mass media, but their response to change was not creative or aggressive in the sense that they sought in any way to alter the existing male system or breach men's traditional territory. Theirs was an alternative, hidden, agenda which did not include men, but did not actively exclude them. It didn't have to – men, if they were aware of it at all, had no desire to be part of it. These women's response was subjective, and essentially passive. It changed their attitudes to their lives, to their expectations and demands. But always they took it for granted that all this would be provided for them within a masculine-biased political and economic framework. After all, popular culture itself was built on a masculine-controlled commercial framework.

For the purposes of clarity, we have to make a rather simplistic distinction here between the ordinary women who were popular culture's first generation of disciples and the second generation, their daughters. This second generation were very different women, young in the Seventies, whose upbringing had been influenced as thoroughly by popular culture as their mothers' had been by the aftermath of the war.

These younger women experienced popular culture differently. Where their mothers had been influenced and inspired by it, the daughters were aware of themselves as consumers of mass culture, and increasingly took control of its content. Records, videos, fashion and advertising gained in importance over television and BBC radio. Young women listened to Radio Luxembourg and Radio Caroline, and a rash of independent broadcasters providing pop music and chatty DJs rather than BBC pundits. More of that later.

The older women's indoctrination, though, was largely through television, radio, and music within the home. Perhaps the difference between the two generations, although they overlapped, was that the older women were using popular culture to learn how to expand their horizons. They wanted to feel safe – and stars like Val Doonican and Max Bygraves made them feel that. Their daughters didn't need to learn anything of the sort; they wanted to enjoy the scope a much wider conception of popular culture offered them for experiment. They took what the older generation learned much further. A huge generation gap opened up between mothers and daughters. Older women, even as they were undergoing internal change, saw their values overturned by the second generation, whose interests were quite different and often antipathetic to their elders'. The first generation could only see the dangers of the unknown, where the second felt quite at home there.

But that does not detract from the enormity of popular

culture's impact on the older generation. This has to be seen in the context of the lives those women lived. Women's expectations then were a reflection of their husband's status and the work he did. They had no status as individuals outside the home beyond this, and had no opportunities to develop as persons in their own right except within the limitations set by their husbands. Their social life probably centred on belonging to women's organisations which then focused strongly on home and family. Perhaps they were also involved in church activities, but their input would be practical – arranging flowers, cleaning, making cakes for sales to boost church funds; they did not normally participate in intellectual or political policy-making.

Their priorities, even if they worked outside the home as cleaners or in a factory or shop, were always domestic. Pursuing their own interests came a long way behind taking the children to school, fetching them, feeding them, picking up a husband from the station if he didn't drive himself in the one family car, cooking for him, ironing his shirt for work the next day. Not that a woman's contribution was not important to the family interests: in the promotion stakes, a man could stand or fall by his wife's domestic skills and efficiency. The wife was implicated in her husband's suitability for climbing the corporate ladder; her backup commitment was essential. But it was always a supportive role. Corporate Man would not be expected to acknowledge the part his wife played; it would make him look weak. On the other hand, his bosses held him entirely responsible if she failed to conform to his company's 'standards'.

We're not talking about ancient history. It's hard to believe the way women expected to live even in the quite recent past. In the late Sixties and Seventies, poor working-class women and children could still be seen scavenging for coal on slag heaps beside the railway line by train travellers on the way north from London to Newcastle or Manchester. Millions of women lived lives of domestic drudgery without expectations of change for the better. What television in particular did for all these women was to give them access to different ways of living, even if only in their dreams. It told them there were choices, even if they didn't see yet how these applied to them. It also gave them something outside their own lives to talk about amongst themselves, escapist conversations about broader experiences they could discuss although they might not believe they would ever share them. That somehow made them seem more real.

This first generation of women whose mindset was changed by popular culture were used to seeing women in the cinema, but not ordinary women like themselves. They saw the female stars on film portrayed as living in a separate, glossy world which seemed to have nothing in common with day to day life for real women. The screen goddesses were alive and rich and living in Hollywood, but they had little to do with the domestic drudges who coveted their untouchable glamour in the worn plush seats of the local cinema. For real ordinary women, playing at empathising with these film stars was pure escapism.

British films of the late Fifties and early Sixties featured women either as blonde bombshells with precariously big bosoms, or as insipid motherhood-fodder in the *Carry On* movies and the *Doctor in the House* series; or as saucy exploiters of male stupidity in the St Trinian's films. In the Sixties James Bond bedded beautiful girls, but never a married woman. That in itself may have promoted a new moral latitude – the women Bond seduced were often the unhappy girlfriends of other people, usually villains. Objections to promiscuity began to seem unreasonable when the women gained by casual sex. Dissatisfied married women watching the films may well have asked each other if virtue really was its own reward.

There was no pretence that Bond women had anything to do with female reality. If he met a married woman, or a mother with children, he would certainly have run. Indeed, the moment he did marry, his wife was doomed; she was dead by the end of the movie. Clearly, by implication, a married man could not remain a hero and a hero was expected to bed women. Much earlier 'Sapper' failed to realise this mistake in his first Bulldog Drummond book, and had Hugh Drummond marry. 'Sapper' regretted this each time he wrote a new Bulldog Drummond yarn – but in those days even fictional wives were not so easily expendable.

The Sixties and early Seventies produced a series of very masculine films, set in industrial heartlands and depicting women as victims, and extraneous in a life lived on male terms. These ground-breaking British films were no doubt a reaction to the superficiality of the Hollywood Dream Machine, but they were also specifically not aimed at entertaining women or a family audience. Nor were they in the least escapist. Women were burdens who caused problems for men; they came between men; they trapped men into acting against their own interests. These films tended to rub women's noses in the gritty sordid misery of their everyday lives, and they showed no way out of this grim, mundane fate. *This Sporting Life*, *Saturday Night and Sunday Morning*, *Alfie*, *Room at the Top*, these were all films about class, which was the predominant male issue of the time. Women were shown incidentally as helpless victims of both men and the social system.

That may have been the overt message of these films, but cumulatively they did affect the way women thought about themselves. They left no doubt in women's minds that there was no help to be had from men, but they did begin to break down the existing requisite for women, respectability. Female filmgoers saw what women were expected to go through to keep their reputations intact in a male context of violence, sex, and anger, and they wanted to learn more about these aspects of reality, albeit at a distance. The value of respectability began to seem questionable as the rewards appeared ever less attractive. Frankly, in popular culture bad girls, even if they weren't blondes, had more fun.

These films did not make women want the lives of the women on film. They could empathise with much of what they saw as a true reflection of their own lives, but that was not what they wanted. They wanted to dream about what might have been. There was nothing in this reality to inspire them.

There was one iconic moment, though, which captured the essence of popular culture's empty promise to ordinary women. It was a brief scene in *Billy Liar*. Julie Christie, long-legged, blonde hair flying free, handbag swinging, walked past a billboard on a derelict city street and suddenly, briefly, it was as though the sun came out for all women, everywhere. Never mind that it was an empty promise: nothing changed for Liz, the character in the film. But this was a rare image to hint at what popular culture could show women about what they could make of their lives simply from adopting the outward image of an inner change of attitude. Christie/Liz looked as though the world was her oyster, and for the women who saw her, it became a real possibility. That fleeting moment in popular culture was hugely empowering. You might say modern women came of age in that brief scene.

Even so, films were not the mind-changing part of popular culture for women that television became. Film was always remote, separated from ordinary women's real-life experience. Films were not constantly available on TV in those days. People went out to the cinema to see them. The point about early popular culture, particularly television, was that the ordinary woman participated in the drama, but in her own territory; her experience of it, especially in soaps and daytime dramas, was a personal relationship between herself as an individual woman and the programme. This was enhanced, incidentally, because television lacked the sophistication of films. The dialogue, settings, and acting in soaps on TV did not have the slickness and expensive gloss found in films. TV dramas often seemed amateurish. But this is what made the actors and what they said and did, as well as where they said it, seem real. The barriers between what was real and what was unreal began to blur.

Early soaps and sitcoms about ordinary life recognised that women viewers en masse had been suffering from a kind of emotional agoraphobia. The programmes played safe. There was always a family-nest familiarity about settings in those early days – the Sugdens' kitchen at Emmerdale Farm, the snug bar of the Rover's Return in *Coronation Street*. This continues, though now it's more to do with a centre of community – the Woolpack in *Emmerdale* and the Queen Vic in *EastEnders*. Wherever, soaps essentially give a heart to a community, much as an Aga does to a home.

TV has a special function in popular culture because it offers a semblance of reality, but deals in unreality. Many women still have trouble telling one from another. They write in large numbers even now to soap opera 'characters' as though they were real people. 'Real' newspapers carried headlines with a campaign 'Free the Weatherfield One' calling for the release from jail of Deirdre Rachid in *Coronation Street*. Prime Minister Tony Blair even raised the case in Parliament. That was certainly the most notorious case of popular culture's blurring the dividing lines between truth and fiction, but certainly not the only one. Soap opera actors frequently find themselves recognised as their fictional characters, which often, in the case of those playing doctors in *Casualty*, for example, involves being asked for their 'professional' advice.

It's a fine dividing line. The *Sun* newspaper ran an interview with an actress about her life-threatening illness which was actually about the cancer of her on-screen character. But who's to say that a number of women who were really in the same position as the fictional sufferer were not encouraged and helped by what she said?

When the media operate in unison like this, with the newspapers and magazines picking up issues covered in TV drama, this does provide women with a chance to test-drive different situations, alternative lifestyles, and modes of behaviour as though they were real. Women led very insulated lives within their own milieu, and *Coronation Street* gave them a 'real' experience of life in backstreet Manchester, or working in a Birmingham motel in *Crossroads*, or rural life in a Yorkshire village in *Emmerdale*. The effect, of course, was to create stereotypes which were not necessarily even close to reality, but it was as near as most women had ever come to sharing their experiences. And also it was not like sharing these experiences with strangers; the TV set brought these other women, these real-seeming fictional characters, into the home as friends.

Better than friends, perhaps. Most women suffered from lack of confidence in themselves. To make real-life friends involved risking rejection, possible embarrassment, and disappointment. If a woman invited other women home, she laid herself open to being judged and found wanting. Her style, her personal belongings, her cooking all came under critical scrutiny. 'TV friends' might invite women viewers to 'judge' them, but at least they did not reciprocate.

The men who stage-managed early popular culture did not consider women specifically as a separate entity to men. They saw no particular potential in women's interests, and despised the intellectual content of the television the mass of women watched. But they were forced to recognise that women, confined to the home, were the majority of their audience. Particularly this was true with the advent of mass day-time television in the Seventies. But neither did the TV programme-makers see any advantage in trying to 'protect' women from what they saw as visual blotting paper for their overactive feelings by improving the standard of the content of the programmes. They were interested in boosting viewing figures, so they gave women what they thought they wanted. And, on the independent channels, pumped out advertising for home-and-children products to boost revenue. They suspected that popular culture would ultimately make women want what they hadn't got if they could stimulate their acquisitiveness. Their task was to exploit a commercial opportunity for the advertisers and, later, even for sponsors.

With hindsight it is extraordinary, considering how fundamental was the effect, how haphazard the process of changing women's outlook seems to have been. Programme makers set out to entertain and to capture mass audiences. Women were numerically an important part of their constituency. But to that end the television companies were forced to be more progressive and liberated in representing ordinary women than they perhaps intended, because, in the words of Bill Podmore, the former *Coronation Street* producer, 'satisfied wives and mothers are boring in drama terms'. He said, 'Marriage so easily diminishes women characters in a serial,' and so most of the main female characters (except for the comic relief) were on their own and also without the burden – in terms of drama – of children.

So to make fictional ordinary women on screen inter-esting to real women viewers, the programme makers had to have more sensational things happen to them than would happen in real life. These more sensational happenings, though, were still restricted to the domestic territory. They couldn't risk becoming out of touch with the women watching them. In effect, that restricted the drama to emotion and psychological angst within domestic relation-ships, with a few disastrous gas explosions or traffic accidents thrown in. But there was endless potential in spicing up the emotional lives of female characters within the essentially 'boring' limitations of marriage and family. There's a range of universally felt emotion within those metaphorical four walls – sex, envy, fear of loss, concern for the future, money worries, perversion, even love. Pluck these strings and there are an infinite range of variations on quite narrow themes for soap scenarios to explore.

Ordinary women became involved in Elsie Tanner's love life or the agonising of a teenage girl facing pregnancy without marriage. I remember a middle-aged woman telling me on a long train journey how she used to rush home from work during her lunch hour to watch *Neighbours*. She had been married for about twenty years, and had two sons in their late teens. Her marriage was not unhappy. But she had met a man, a younger man who worked with her husband, who had made her suddenly aware that she was disappointed and bored with her life and what she had made of herself. At the time there was a character in *Neighbours*, a woman called Maria, who was agonising over whether she should leave her Ramsay Street husband and her sons for a man she had met and fallen in love with. The stranger on the train was convinced that this fictional storyline was telling her what to do in her real life. She dared not miss an episode. When Maria did leave her family, this woman felt an overwhelming sense of relief because somehow it permitted her to do what she realised she had wanted all along. She admitted that the *Neighbours* story gave her the courage to leave and join her new love. Not for love, which was incidental, but because seeing what seemed to be her own life on television showed her how unfulfilled she felt in her marriage. The new lover gave her an assisted passage out. She also said that the possibility of leaving had not even occurred to her until she saw the *Neighbours* storyline; without that, she said, she would never have acted on what the new man had made her feel. But after she went, she had gone on watching *Neighbours*. Any guilt she felt about what she had done to her husband and children was assuaged as the abandoned Ramsay Street family gradually recovered from their shock and became happier and wiser people for the emotional experience. 'They gave me permission,' she said.

Interestingly, the women who got involved in these soap story lines were usually encouraged to be on the side of the woman prepared to leave her 'duties' as wife and mother to take a chance on happiness. That was inevitably popular culture's message, because it led to drama and emotional conflict. And the men these women left were almost always the bad guys. Not necessarily violent or cruel, but taking the woman for granted, unappreciative, and insensitive to her needs. These men were also boring, which is the Sin Against the Holy Ghost in popular culture terms. The message beamed into millions of homes was that husbands did not deserve their wives. Ordinary women were being given permission to consider their own interests. They were being told they had a choice.

What this amounted to had a political construction for women. It gave them an awareness that they did not have to see themselves as victims. Or rather popular culture could make them believe that even if they were victims in the real world, they could use their victimhood to their own advantage. They were not helpless, and if they did not like the situation they were in, they could change it. Very few of them would, of course; they were wives and mothers and they had been brought up to see their female role as a duty. That duty was based on feeling, it wasn't rational. Popular culture promised them that choosing emotion over reason empowered them.

Television also offered a kind of underlying impression that if a woman tried to fly and broke her wings, she would be looked after. On TV, kindly older uncle figures like Robert Dougall took fear of the unknown out of the news of the day; Richard Dimbleby left no doubt that he was in charge of great events and nothing would go wrong on his watch; Malcolm Muggeridge would always be able to draw the sting of anyone who threatened the stability of the wider world. In *Emergency Ward Ten*, personable young doctors listened sympathetically to women's woes, and *Dixon of Dock Green* made women feel safer on the streets. This was an important factor in women's relationship with what they saw on television. It was crucial to the way they responded to Dixon, to Inspector Wexford, Morse, Bergerac, among others. All these series gave women a glimpse of something ugly about real life – murder, revenge, madness – and then took the bad taste away by making our brave heroes defeat such evils. These were all early stirrings of the guardian role popular culture itself would later take on in women's lives.

John Fiske wrote, in *Television Culture* (1987), 'Soap operas keep patriarchy under constant interrogation, they legitimise feminine values and thus produce self-esteem for the women who live by them. They provide, in short, the means for a feminine culture . . . '

I would go further. I think soaps – and much more that women saw on television – actually created new feminine values, as opposed to the prevailing male-dominated value system previously set out for them by the masculine hierarchies. Because of the demand for sensationalism and melodrama, they seemed to give permission to women to loose social conventions and to judge outrageous behaviour by different criteria than they were used to applying in their own lives. But this was early days in mass popular culture and there was a long way to go before women were really confident about what they had learned.

At this stage, humour on television too played an important part. Women were used to being put down by male comedians joking to mainly male audiences about nagging wives and interfering mothers-in-law. Suddenly, on prime time television, women comedians like Marti Caine and Victoria Wood stood up and laughed at themselves for being silly *women*; they laughed at men, too, and millions of women laughed with them for the first time as a female entity at the basic absurdity of their traditional oppressors. And also at the absurdity of their own collusion with them. Watching women comics – or even men in drag – being funny about the female condition helped ordinary women face the fears that had held them back from contemplating change. Fears of making fools of themselves, of not being sexually attractive, of being alone and unsupported – women standing on their own feet in comedy series like *Rhoda*, *Cybill*, *Roseanne* all helped beat such bogeys.

With hindsight today, we can trace a historical thread developing from what we learn about women's changing lives in the way they were portrayed on TV from the 1960s through the Nineties. Take *Dallas*, through *Dynasty*, to *Desperate Housewives* – pampered hobby-job wives turn into boardroom sex sirens and then into self-preserving manipulators who move men around like chess pieces.

Another obvious shift is illustrated by considering TV programmes' attitude to older women. In the early days of *Coronation Street*, for instance, Ena Sharples seemed to encompass a lifetime of experience which made her worthy of respect. She acted as a commentator on ethical and social questions arising from other people's actions. Annie Sugden in *Emmerdale* had a similar function. Today, that TV stereotype is gone; now older women live by the same standards and expectations as the young, and in their efforts to compete sexually, become grotesque.

Increasingly over the decades, the tool of all women's trade on TV is perceived as sex. It is what they do with it that has changed, from early days of aspiring to be in love to today's cold-blooded manipulation to achieve some kind of (probably material) satisfaction.

There are deeper implications to all this. Television helped to introduce 'mass' society. It was seen as a threat to traditional literary culture which emphasised individual discrimination. As a mass medium it took on the capacity to destabilise the hierarchical status quo. Indeed, many early pundits – half the Cabinet at the time of the Queen's coronation to name a few – saw the development of television as a threat to the traditions of society itself. They feared that popular culture would make people discontented and fuel envy. As a mass medium addressing an audience not defined by class or education or money, but, predominantly, by gender, they thought that even if not dangerously anarchic in its influence, it would disrupt accepted social conventions. From the start many were afraid of where it might lead because they could see that it would be difficult to control its mass audience from outside. Indeed, the avowed priority of many pioneers of mass television culture was to overturn the class structure. As far as women were concerned, though, it's more likely that programme-makers' intention was never to make women happy; they were after a kind of dummy that would keep them quiet. They already foresaw that popular culture was where power would lie. They just had not yet realised that it was women who would be empowered.

5

But television was not alone in its effect. Other aspects of the popular-culture media began to feed off one another to create an empire of commercial self-interest where they allowed women to feel in control.

Books were not, of course, part of the embryonic new mass technology as television was. Stories, written down or told, go back centuries to the days when Scheherazade told her tales on a Thousand and One Nights to beguile and finally enlighten the murderous King of Samarkand who had vowed to kill her and a thousand virgins one by one. A real man's man, the old King.

Educated women who could read had enjoyed novels for centuries. In Britain there were best-selling popular novels for a quasi-mass readership in the 1790s when, in *Northanger Abbey*, Jane Austen made fun of Mrs Radcliffe's *Mysteries of Udolpho*. Charlotte Brontë (as Currer Bell) wrote novels for and about women, as did Mary Ann Evans (as George Eliot). Men also wrote about women, too, without having to hide their identity behind noms de plume, Benjamin Disraeli among them. It is interesting, though, that Flaubert, in publishing *Madame Bovary*, became a *cause célèbre* for flouting public decency because he suggested that any normal ordinary woman would behave as poor Emma did. Emma was also brave, Flaubert defended her, because she dared to live out her dreams, like Don Quixote. Later, Flaubert had to retract this, saying the book was a warning to immoral women.

John Cleland also ran into trouble, being forced to withdraw *Fanny Hill: Memoirs of a Woman of Pleasure* when he and his publisher were charged with 'corrupting the King's subjects'.

This suggests that the established authorities were always afraid of the sensational aspects of popular culture, concerned that the public, and in particular, impressionable women, might enjoy it too much and be led astray. They feared that this could damage family life and result in social breakdown. Men have always had problems facing the real nature of their women, and in acknowledging that they are not fully in control of female emotions.

At least in the case of *Fanny Hill*, popular culture emerged victorious at last when women's appetite for its sensation and passion created commercial demand. There were several expurgated versions of *Fanny Hill* published in the late-eighteenth and nineteenth centuries, but it was not until 1963 that an unexpurgated paperback hit the mass market. The police prosecuted, and won, but the revealed gulf between the obscenity laws and social realities in late 60s Britain changed outdated attitudes and in 1970 an un-expurgated edition was published without trouble. Women's increasing involvement in demand for popular mass-market books had become a political consideration in forcing change on a legal system which was beginning to look oudated.

That publication was in paperback is important. In the commercial books market, inexpensive paperback editions fuelled its potential as part of popular culture. Though Penguin had pioneered cheap paperback editions of classic books in the 1930s, and other publishers followed, it was the Second World War that provided a breakthrough.

Soldiers bought these compact versions of popular novels to carry in their pockets and read when they could; shift workers in the factories did the same. Needs must, and women forced by rationing and restrictions on travel to stay at home in the evenings spent more time reading.

Paperbacks brought books into the mass market. The story of Mills & Boon illustrates this. The publisher was founded in 1908. In the 1930s, the company began to specialise in romance in response to the market for escapism during the Depression. The books were sold through weekly two-penny libraries and were always intended to cater for a wide readership. Then, when the lending libraries began to decline in the late 1950s, the company produced cheap editions of its romances sold through newsagents throughout the country. In popular culture terms, that's important too. Newsagents offer easier access to women in the street than bookshops. Mills & Boon has more than three million regular readers in the UK every year.

The same strategy – selling paperbacks outside the traditional booksellers – led to a boom in sales after the Sixties. This was when the concept of cheap package holidays began to take off, and people bought these books at bookstalls in the airports to amuse themselves while they waited for their flights. Supermarkets, too, were springing up in every town, and they, too, sold mass-market paperback books. It was very easy for women to pick up a cheap paperback with their shopping.

We have seen that the early impact of television was to give ordinary women emotional access to the lives of other women similar to themselves. If TV showed women what they could do and be, new cheap popular fiction written by women explored what happens next.

Catherine Cookson, in true popular-culture fashion, produced exactly the bestselling novels which took the mass of women another step towards political empowerment.

If some mogul of popular culture had been looking for a real-life metaphor for what would capture the state of the psyche of ordinary women at the time, he would have invented Catherine Cookson. Her real-life story had all the ingredients that defined popular culture. She was brought up by her grandparents in grim, deprived South Shields, believing her unmarried mother was her sister. She struggled to make a living, married, and took in lodgers to earn money. She suffered four miscarriages and a nervous breakdown. Then she started to write.

She wrote about a woman's world co-existing with but different from a man's. From the early Sixties she published a hundred novels, concentrating on women ground down by circumstances who use the resources of their own characters to break out and overcome adversity. For twenty years she was the most borrowed author from libraries. One hundred and twenty three million copies of her novels have been sold to date. For millions of women, clearly, the medium was the message they wanted to hear. For ordinary women struggling towards their own identity within a hostile social system, novels like these were empowering.

Catherine Cookson's novels were categorised as romantic fiction. She took issue with that label, but the books she wrote were rags-to-riches stories about women whose emotional, if not actual, circumstances resonated with her readers. The preconceptions of the time tended to see all mass-market novels catering for a female readership as romantic fiction; perhaps this was less because they involved romantic love than because their plots were escapist and unlikely to happen often in real life. In real life, the fictional heroine's initiative and independence would be thwarted before it got off the ground by women's perceived submissive role in society.

But ordinary women were already living their real lives partly in another dimension created for them by popular culture. This was a dimension where they could escape the actual performance of everyday demands made on them by family and community into a dream world where they would be indulged and cared for and able to live for themselves. 'Light' literature aimed at women enabled them to see popular culture's dreamworld as unrealistic but also, exceptionally, as possible.

Catherine Cookson's novels were not genre romantic fiction because they had a central love interest and a happy ending. They were also inspirational, specifically urging women towards empowerment. As popular culture, they were overtly political in the way they encouraged women towards change.

Yes, inexpensive paperback editions brought books into the realms of popular culture, and the commercial interests behind them aimed them at a female market. They concentrated on the two genres read and written largely by women – romance and crime fiction.

These essentially deal with two areas where the focus of women's lives was changing most significantly – sexuality and aggression.

Much has been written at an academic level about how Mills & Boon has been forced to adapt its formulae in the face of feminism. Lovers now are forced to go to once undreamed of acts of passion to fulfil readers' demands. A collection of essays published in the 1980s, *The Progress of Romance*, also claims that the genre has found it increasingly necessary to engage specifically with feminism. Feminism, though, can mean simply women who have been politically empowered, but not necessarily by an intellectual intention to implement feminist policy. Romantic fiction now needs a working, independent heroine even while disparaging the women's movement itself, usually through the speeches of the hero, who, of course, learns better. But however imperfect, the hero cannot be dispensed with; he is invariably the lead player in a happy ending for the heroine. But he probably needed to mend his ways over the years, if one of Mills & Boon's writers, Violet Winspear, was right in 1970 when she wrote that all her heroes had to be 'capable of rape'.

In the best traditions of escapist literature, though, Mills & Boon romances adhere to the criteria of popular culture. There is always a happy ending, they are written very simply, and the plots are predictable. This last is what research shows that fans say they like about the books. Familiarity breeds content. Romantic fiction readers have this in common with readers of pornography. Publishers apparently instruct authors of porn to lift a third of their previous book and use it virtually word for word in a current story: it seems this makes the reader feel at home. In romantic fiction, where every variation has a similar happy ending, the repetition must reassure the avid reader that art might mirror reality.

For ordinary women, the love-struggle in popular romantic fiction has always been part of the larger struggle for their right to define and control their own sexuality. This is a new departure for many of them, and romantic fiction gives them access to information about what is involved. This is part of the bestseller factor for a wide range of popular writers – Mary Wesley, Jilly Cooper, and Joanna Trollope included. Perhaps it also helps to explain why women devour a particular author's books for a while and then move on to someone else, a new favourite author. Readers take out of a romantic novel what corresponds to their emotional need at the time; once they have worked through that aspect of their feelings, the urge to a new sensation drives them to try something new.

And, of course, romantic fiction always has an optimistic message for readers – Janice Radway wrote in *Reading the Romance* (1984): 'I find it impossible to ignore that romance reading creates a feeling of hope, provides emotional sustenance and produces a visceral sense of well-being . . . romance reading, it appears, addresses needs, desires and wishes that a male partner could not.' And she links reading this genre with a message to ordinary women: 'I see romance reading as a form of individual resistance to a situation predicated on the assumption that it is women alone who are responsible for the care and emotional nurturance of others. Romance reading buys time and privacy for women even as it addresses the corollary consequences of their situation, the physical exhaustion and emotional depletion brought about by the fact that no-one within the patriarchal family is charged with *their* care.'

This is another area where feminists missed an opportunity to get in touch with what was actually happening in ordinary women's heads. Scornful of its undemanding lack of intellectual content and its 'popularity', they tended to dismiss the genre as escapist, unrealistic, absurd and manipulative of women. The solutions of women's emotional sufferings in these stories is certainly facile, and in real life would offer no solution at all. Some have suggested that romance readers seek to regress in the hero/heroine relationship to the time in their own lives when they were the focus of their mother's care. The theory goes that the romance thus provides a way for them to experience vicariously the emotional nurture they are expected to give to others. Perhaps the feminists were justified in trying to wean women from this perception that they can only be happy and fulfilled in this role. Their criticism of romantic fiction, however, appears patronising. It also makes them seem elitist. The popularity of the genre shows that it provides something that the mass of women want. In the 1970s, the growth of feminism was mirrored almost exactly by a boom in the popularity of romance novels.

Here again, as in what they watch on television, women's sexuality is made safe in these stories because they experiment within a secure world where they know that a man will provide ultimate succour. Whatever the imperfections of the hero at the start – and this can include rudeness, cruelty, even sexual violence – the heroine always manages to bring him to a state of grace which makes him a safe marital bet. Romances suggest that the woman's power lies in her sexuality, and how, by submitting to her lover, she can control the way he treats her. That dubious popular culture premise is, it seems, what living happily ever after means.

Romantic fiction empowered the woman reader because, by identifying with the heroine of the story, she is made to feel that in expressing her sexuality she is in ultimate control of the man she chooses to love. These stories do not tell her that there is nothing to fear from the sexuality of men; they do reassure her that if she makes wise choices, she can 'tame' male sensuality and will reap considerable reward in terms of a happy relationship.

There is a fundamental problem here for feminists, that for most ordinary women what is attractive about the hero are the very macho characteristics which rule him out as partner to an empowered woman. Romantic novels, as all forms of popular culture, make clear that ultimately the choice is hers. Real or not, to generations of women whose expectation and experience was that men chose and women made the best of it, this comes as an enlightening revelation.

Romantic fiction told women that they could contain the violence and cruelty innate in men's sexuality within a relationship, but this was no answer to the growing rage and brute force that increasingly pervaded society as a whole. This anger was not exclusive to men. Women, too, needed to express their anger and frustration.

Popular culture contributed to women's awareness of the violence within them by whipping up emotion through melodrama, and helping these women identify with each other on an intense level of feeling. As a by-product, there was now an emotional market for catharsis to express anger.

This demand led to new departures in crime fiction. The old-fashioned macho stuff – Bulldog Drummond, James Bond, even Philip Marlowe – where the hero and villains alike slug it out physically didn't do it for women; slugging it out was never their forte. The best-selling crime fiction which appealed to women has had the effect of helping them to face the violence inherent in both male and female.

Violence is inevitable where human beings live too closely together. Over centuries of learned submission, it was expedient for women to suppress the violence they felt. Their comparative physical weakness taught them to fear their own and others' aggression. As popular culture made women more aware of themselves as individuals, and more demanding of attention, their innate aggression towards social systems and people who did not recognise their needs had to seek an outlet. New mass market crime fiction written for and by women from the Seventies helped them define their own needs and, also, gave them access through sensation and melodrama to the authenticity of female anger within society as a whole. It provided catharsis for their feelings, but also a framework to contain violence.

Crime stories gave women the chance, in their own time and a safe environment, to confront physical fear of the world outside the home; popular culture in this form built up women's confidence in themselves to express aggression and anger. The genre also helped women who had been programmed to see their comparative weakness as an advantage to question the disadvantages of being a protected species, with all the restrictions this involved.

In a 1944 essay on the crime writer James Hadley Chase, author of *No Orchids for Miss Blandish*, George Orwell noted the emergence during the war of a new realism in crime writing. What he said then about a very macho genre seems to me relevant to women and the crime fiction they were reading in the Sixties and Seventies. He defined the new realism he was writing about as 'Realism meaning the doctrine that might is right. The growth of realism has been the great feature of the intellectual history of our age . . . the interconnection between sadism, masochism, success-worship, power-worship, nationalism and totalitarianism is a huge subject . . . '

Once popular culture made it possible for women to take in that in real life might is apparently perceived as right, they could then start to process their fears and counteract that reality.

That trend is mirrored in earlier stages of women's crime writing. Compare Dorothy L. Sayers' Harriet Vane, a feisty New Woman of the Twenties, with the tough heroines of Sue Grafton or Sara Paretsky. Harriet Vane, an intelligent and independent young woman, is often irritated at herself because she needs to call upon the support of Lord Peter Wimsey, but she accepts that she does. It's quite clear, throughout *Strong Poison* (1930) and *Have His Carcase* (1932), for example, that a violent reaction is not an option for women, unless, as in *Gaudy Night* (1935), there is no prospect of physical retaliation. Indeed, *Gaudy Night* is a rare crime novel in that it has no murder.

At the very least, Lord Peter offers Harriet physical protection, and, incidentally, he also provides a way round social restrictions laid on women at the time by giving her access to male hierarchies closed to her as a female on her own.

Sue Grafton and Sara Paretsky, on the other hand, have women protagonists who are not afraid or unable to take violent action if necessary. That is an important resource when the new villains (men with power, wealth, influence) can usually claim openly to have right on their side simply because they have might. It has also to be noted that both these writers are American. The legal use in America of handguns makes men and women much more equal physically; in theory anyway. When George Orwell was talking about the new realism in crime-writing during the war, he stressed that though James Hadley Chase, the subject of his essay, was born English he wrote 'American'.

Crime writers like Paretsky and Grafton with their action-women protagonists, give their readers the chance, in their own time, to confront physical fear of the world outside the home; and the confidence to express their own aggression and anger by allying themselves with these heroines against villains who are less individuals than metaphors for aspects of the masculine status quo. These heroines show women that they do not have to be helpless. They have a choice. The genre has also, perhaps, led women to question the disadvantages of being a protected species, with all the restrictions involved.

This is a far cry from the classic English sleuth Miss Marple, for instance, although Agatha Christie was herself half-American. Miss Marple is precluded from physical action because of age, so she is in a position of weakness vis-à-vis the criminal. She is ultimately protected by her nephew Raymond, and by policemen who are forced to recognise that the Marple feminine wiles succeed where male brute force and ignorance do not. Jane Marple's weapons are the traditional female strengths, the lateral thinking, psychology and intuition of the feminine mind. These crime stories, even though they extended to the 1970s, were from the pre-popular-culture age but they do have a message to ordinary women that they should not despise their female resources. The closest Miss Marple comes to aggressive action is to set herself up in a passive role as bait to draw the villain out to reveal himself. Or, in *The Body in the Library* (1942), herself; even Agatha Christie offers female villains. It's rare that such women act alone without male support, but 'bad' women are prepared to use physical violence against a male invalid or another woman.

Surprisingly a very early Christie heroine, Tuppence, in the Tommy and Tuppence stories which started in the

1920s, is closer to being an early version of Grafton's Kinsey Millhone or Paretsky's V. I. Warshawski. The crimes in which Tuppence plays an important part move away from the villagey cosiness of Miss Marple. Even so when Tommy and Tuppence take on a nest of dangerous spies there is still a distinction between the male and the female in the way they operate. In extremis, Tommy acts more macho, Tuppence tends to fall back on her helpless femininity. The femininity is usually more effective. This gender distinction is lost by the time crime writing became a mass-market facet of popular culture's process of women's empowerment. Nor was that empowerment any less important because these new writers were American, and wrote about American women. Popular culture in Britain was always, and is still, the end-product of a process that includes the rest of the English-speaking world.

In the Tommy and Tuppence books, starting with *The Secret Adversary* (1922), there is no ambivalence about the villains and the wrong-ness of what they do. Whereas in the later crime writers featuring women of action, villains can be admired as long as they are successful. The reader is not escaping her mundane routine into an imaginary world of action, but rather into a world of cruelty and perversion. Crime fiction, in acknowledging this world and revealing it, awakened a long-submerged, emotionally localised, power instinct in women.

When Kinsey Millhone or V. I. Warshawski or Patricia Cornwell's Kay Scarpetta face this instinct in themselves and harness it to win out against wrong-doing, they become significant role models for women to throw off dependence. And this is not just physical dependence; it includes acceptance of black and white moral standards set by a social system which was fast becoming outdated and irrelevant. The new women's crime fiction allowed ordinary women to make their own judgements about what is good and bad. Here the melodramatic and sentimental excesses of popular culture begin to show their effects. Moral shades of good and bad now begin to reflect, not absolute judgements like right and wrong, but elements of what has brought the character to villainy. A murder victim can perhaps have contributed when alive to the reasons he is killed; a killer bullied at school who takes revenge on his former tormenters is not as 'bad' as a paedophile.

Popular culture has introduced an element of degrees of blame, where society itself, and everyone in it, becomes implicated in any violent crime. And the corollary to that – a message particularly empowering to women who have less access to expressing physical violence – is the strength to be gained from reacting as a group. This grouping need not be actual, it is notional. It is the weight of female public opinion, and it is a new departure for women. Popular culture has taken another step towards politicising the mass of women.

6

The mass appeal of best-selling paperback books was not the written word's only sector of popular culture which was indoctrinating ordinary women with its empowering messages. The effect of what was happening in newspapers and magazines was probably even more significant because they gave a political voice to female public opinion.

'Handbook' novels were teaching women how to cope with the new directions their lives were taking. The books of Barbara Taylor Bradford and Jilly Cooper, for example, have in common only that they show ordinary women who turn unpromising starts into uniquely feminine success. Barbara Taylor Bradford – *A Woman of Substance* (1979), *Hold the Dream* (1985) – concentrates on the business arena, while Jilly Cooper's early heroines – *Emily* (1975), *Prudence* (1978) – tend to be shy and unsophisticated ugly ducklings who turn into swans to win the hearts of their heroes.

Best-selling novels like these hint at the changes that are going on in ordinary women's attitudes. What this kind of fiction was saying was reflected simultaneously on television in series like *Dallas* and characters like Alexis Colby in *Dynasty*. Britain's own contribution to the direction popular culture was taking came in TV series like *The Brothers* and *Howard's Way*, where extremely feminine women use their sexuality to bypass by stealth male machinations. Pundits like to talk about such women – particularly the 'evil' Alexis – as more macho in her business dealings than any man. It isn't true; Alexis was simply more female than ordinary women dared to be. Women were not expected to dislike her because of what she did to men. Surely then she would have been hailed as a heroine. They disliked her because of the way she treated other women. Popular culture had created a feeling of solidarity amongst ordinary women; as one of popular culture's most successful creations, Joan Collins's Alexis betrayed the community of women, and that's why she was a villain.

Television and mass-market fiction were changing women's perceptions and expectations but it was a somewhat subliminal, even accidental, process. In newspapers and magazines, though, the intention to give these women a political platform was overt and deliberate.

TV and novels as mass change-agents dealt in fiction; newspapers then dealt in facts, and in newspapers, women were becoming news. Features concentrated on ordinary women expressing awareness of their new empowerment to break into male fields of operation – pilots, merchant navy officers, blacksmiths et al. These women were pioneering individuals, but by publicising their feats, the newspapers made sure they became role models for the masses.

The reason for this was very simple. Money.

This deliberate targeting of ordinary women started from the late Sixties and 1970s when they became economically important. The baby boom caused a glut of young women who expected to work until they married and settled down. They were not, in the main, dedicated career women; they wanted money so that they could have as much fun as possible while they were young and carefree. That is, they wanted to spend not on the promises of the male Establishment, on pensions or insurance or investments, but with the ephemeral delights that popular culture would provide.

Of course the vast commercial interests behind popular culture licked their corporate lips in glee. These young women offered an infinite new market to exploit through the ever increasing penetration of all aspects of popular culture into everyday life. And, given the undemanding and simplistic nature of popular culture, the development of this new growth market carried no limitations of broad-based social responsibility.

Newspapers and magazines embraced the Live Now, Pay Later mentality amongst young women at the time. Popular culture had brought them the confidence to make such choices for themselves, and en masse they opted for the gratifications of sensation, pleasure and image while there was still time. The nuclear bomb and the Cold War brought ever closer the reality of the world ending, but there was nothing the mass of ordinary young women could do about it. Protest marches and spectacular love-ins in themselves became part of popular culture. All they knew to use as weapons in their own defence was a form of popular culture itself; image without substance, passion without thought.

Under such a cataclysmic threat of annihilation, the only form of effective defiance at the state of the real world was to cram as much sensation as possible into what time there was left before annihilation or marriage and children forced them back into the real world. What their mothers had seen as a launch pad for the start of their real lives was perceived by the daughters as the end of their life as discrete individuals and the start of a kind of dehumanised existence living for – and through – others. Of course they crammed what time they had for themselves with pleasure, sensation and entertainment. Why not? After all, what harm could they do? Theirs was surely a victimless source of pleasure.

It was also a licence to print money.

In the late Sixties and early Seventies the popular newspapers embraced the increasing importance of women as a potential source of profit on two fronts: circulation, and advertising revenue.

The mass-market dailies were locked in a bitter circulation war. At the tabloid end of the market, the competition was fierce as each tried to outdo the others with pictures of topless girls and sexually titillating stories, all in an effort to woo traditional male readers. The *Daily Mirror* did make some effort to go upmarket, but after the *Sun* was launched in 1964 it abandoned such pretension and returned to the traditional format.

But that was designed to appeal to an ageing male readership dependent on constant replenishment by time, not new growth. Newspapers were running out of money and disappearing. The *Daily Herald* went, and then the *Daily Sketch*. They did not know how to break with their tried and true macho formulae, or look outside the readership they knew and understood. When the *Herald*, which had long been associated with the Trades Union Congress and the working man, was forced to close, it was still one of the top 20 circulations in the world. Its problem was that it could not attract advertising.

There was, however, a potential virgin market to win over. It included the working and lower middle class women whose lives and expectations had been expanded by popular culture. This new constituency of ordinary women who wanted to see their own interests reflected in the newspapers represented a viable opportunity for real growth.

These women's interests were different from the traditional pages for 'the ladies' which the newspapers had always included as a sop to their readers' wives. Those had focused on domestic issues, on manners and children and the home, all within the context of life in a patriarchal family. Now women were no longer content to read the women's pages of their husbands' newspaper. They looked to buy a paper of their own, and they were the consumers influenced by the advertising which was becoming a more and more important source of newspaper revenue.

As we have seen, the *Daily Herald* with its dyed-in-the-wool male working-class readership, died from lack of advertising revenue. The advertising industry was used to targeting women in magazines and on TV, but they were largely aimed at selling domestic goods and focused on family life – Bisto gravy, Whiter than White washing powders, that kind of thing.

In the late Seventies representatives of the advertising department of Peugeot cars attended a working lunch at the *Guardian*. I was there as the reporter covering the motor industry. One of the men asked, 'Why are you here? Cars are a man's world. Men buy cars.'

But advertisers (including Peugeot) were beginning to recognise that women were playing an increasing part in choices of non-domestic items. Their input was important in decisions about buying cars or holidays or houses, not least because they were probably helping to pay for them. What attracted women to a product, though, was not the same thing as appealed to men. The advertisers had to make a commercial decision to start targeting women specifically.

The new women's issues concentrated on female sexuality and gender mores. There was a new generation of single young women with money to spend looking for representation in newspapers. They had money and they wanted to go out and enjoy themselves. Newspaper editors like Hugh Cudlipp of the *Daily Mirror* and David English of the *Daily Mail* set about changing the whole concept of women's interests as domestic and maternal to reflect the preoccupations of these younger women. Entertainers and entertainment became more prominent, along with fashion and shopping to attract the growth market which brought in advertising.

The more successful newspapers began to take on a kind of mentor role aimed at women readers. The hard news aspect in the tabloids became less prominent. News coverage itself reflected the growing perception that women were more interested in what was happening in health and behavioural psychology and in human issues than they were in concepts and ideas. Agony aunts and advice columns dealt with sexual and relationship problems, and dropped questions of social etiquette in favour of advice on how to look and behave to attract men. Popular culture had helped young women to see themselves as peer groups. They were interested in what other women in the peer group they belonged to were doing, what they wore, what they ate, who did their hair. Joanna Lumley became a popular-culture icon in the mid-seventies as Purdey in *The New Avengers* because of her haircut.

Editors began to employ women journalists to write features with a wider brief than the domestic arena in order to cater for the preoccupations of their new younger readership. These were single women who earned their own money and lived in bedsitters or shared flats with other girls like themselves and spent their leisure (literally) by going out and experimenting with all that popular culture offered. There was a spate of flatshare series on TV, like *The Liver Birds, Girls on Top,* and even including painfully young-at-heart over-50s in *The Golden Girls.* Journalist Katharine Whitehorn became a bestseller with her book *Cooking in a Bedsitter,* and in the 1990s Helen Fielding's novel based on her newspaper column *Bridget Jones's Diary* tapped into the market of young, free, women who took their identity from their peer groups.

So where did the mass circulation newspapers look for these new-style women journalists? Those educated feminist women who had gone into the media to seek political power had not disappeared. Nor had they diluted their revolutionary ideals. As newspapers and magazines became a potential political platform, they took jobs on papers and magazines they would not have read themselves because they saw an opportunity to promote women's issues against men. This included the newspapers' traditional male readerships, but it also involved manipulating what the newspaper stood for. In the Fifties, women's pages in newspapers were given over to what male executives saw as women's interests as submissive wives and mothers. But the new ambitious feminists working for these men were determined to expand the areas of interest covered and to confront previously taboo subjects for women – like promiscuity and single parenthood – for political ends. Newspaper editors, who had previously let their wives set the agenda when it came to women's interests, found the new ambitious feminists working for them were highly motivated career women who could now compete on equal terms with men because they had the new commercially crucial mass constituency of women to refer to. For once, the issues and the mass market coincided.

This worked very well for an upmarket broadsheet daily like the *Guardian*. The feminists provided a highly articulate platform from which to launch a united female attack on male institutions and hierarchies. But the *Guardian* readership was not representative of ordinary women. The paper always struggled for circulation, and increasingly in public perception the women's pages became a feminist ghetto. What general popular appeal it had outside the feminist movement was in the elements that could be seen to make fun of hard-line feminism, as in Posy's affectionate cartoons lampooning stereotypes of *Guardian* women readers – and writers.

The newspaper which more closely represented ordinary women's interests was the *Daily Mail*. In tune with its new female-orientated agenda, it tended to be features-led. In true popular-culture style, it was politically pragmatic, but never subversive. Editor David English was among the first to appoint a woman features editor who had hands-on experience as a news reporter rather than a university degree. Anthea Disney was directly connected with the ordinary woman (or Mrs Cannybody, as newspaper editors in the provinces liked to call her), whereas the quasi-intellectual feminists never actually knew or understood her.

David English had also been behind Anthea Disney's most powerful stories as a news reporter. She had agreed to his plan to undergo treatment that would darken her skin so that she passed as a coloured immigrant. For months she underwent exactly what black Asian women were enduring in Britain at the time, sharing the rejection of bigoted landladies and prejudice on the streets and trying to get work. It was a defining moment in the emerging new, female-orientated journalism, forcing readers to confront the realities of other people's lives in the Britain of the day.

It is significant that David English chose a woman to do this. He could easily have used a man, whose story might have been equally sensational. But he didn't, and it was the fact that men as well as women were forced to acknowledge the way society treated ethnic-minority women that increased the story's impact. A man's experience might have driven a wedge between the people involved. Men would have justified their own prejudice with some kind of quasi-reasoning that they were defending their traditional way of life against a perceived threat. But being forced to share a woman's experience – a woman who was seen as intrinsically vulnerable – drove men to examine some of the implications in their own treatment of women. And women who might not have tried to question attitudes between men felt a powerful emotional involvement with what was actually happening to one of their own That is probably the first overt, very public, acknowledgement that women were a political force with the potential to bring about change in established male-orientated attitudes in society.

David English recognised very early that women's interests would gain in political importance. He set out to empower ordinary women simply by deliberately catering for such a broad and extensive constituency of female readers that they could not be ignored.

Certainly this process had to do with brainwashing. For the staff, there was no freedom of expression outside his policy. He controlled what went into the paper, editing features personally so that there could be no deviation from the party line he was selling. He used editorial to make women want what his advertisers wanted to sell them. With huge events like the Daily Mail Ideal Home Exhibition, he came close to making the newspaper part of a retailing process. He also brought a new kind of female-biased indignation into news coverage. A definite sympathy towards women began to emerge in stories about crime or work or family life. He presented women as victims, who needed to tap into the consciousness of women like themselves to gain a political voice. Victimhood had moved on from the old concepts of domestic servitude. David English's 'victim women' gained empowerment en masse by the way he could manipulate female public opinion in their defence wherever he felt a female issue merited it and would pay dividends in increased sales.

For the first time, this forced not only the male newspaper executives who sought to exploit the trend, but also men working with women and even in the home, to make more effort to listen to women themselves to find out what they wanted. English made it unacceptable for men to ride roughshod over women's feelings simply by taking a line that showed traditional macho behaviour as exploitive or damaging to a large victim constituency – in so far as you do it unto me, you do it unto others.

In newspapers, always desperate for revenue, the effect of this power base for women inevitably involved trying to tempt them into new areas of interest which would create fresh retail markets. Newspapers and the new women's magazines which were starting up all promoted shopping, fashion, interior design and travel as aspects of popular culture which set out to create demand for new ways for women to spend money on pleasure and to satisfy sensation-seeking.

Women's magazines, also, embraced an educational and consciousness-raising role for the mass female market. They set out to expand the skills and confidence of their growing readerships who were waking to the possibility of breaking through barriers they had long taken for granted from the fact of being female – fair pay for their work, the ability to make independent social, sexual and moral choices. The magazines also expanded popular culture into areas not previously used for propaganda purposes, such as health and beauty. That these are today significant elements of female politics is due to pressure created through popular culture rather than mainstream politics. Certainly feminism wanted nothing to do with what it perceived as male exploitation of femininity.

Of all the magazines aimed at ordinary women *Cosmopolitan* is probably the one which most directly set out to push the boundaries of women's sensuality and, indeed, to politicise their sexuality.

It wasn't the only one. There was the brilliant *Nova*, but *Nova* was frankly too intelligent and cerebral to be popular with ordinary women. It survived for ten years, but it was expensive to produce and run, and the circulation was never more than 100,000. It never made a profit.

Cosmopolitan had originally been an American general-interest magazine, not specifically a women's magazine. Then Helen Gurley Brown took it over with the declared intention of showing young single women who indulged in pre-marital sex that they were not alone. A UK edition was launched in the early Seventies and became enormously successful. It reflected exactly the mood and interests of the new generation of young women in Britain at the time.

Other well-established women's magazines, also, like

Woman and *Women's Own*, now expanded their traditional criteria about what did and what did not interest women. They embraced a role which went well beyond domesticity and maternity without ever becoming feminist. They still stood by the old values of the male hierarchies, but encouraged women to take a more active, positive view of change without actual revolution.

They also set out to expand the skills and confidence of their growing readerships of women who were now alive to the possibility of adapting the barriers they had long taken for granted from the fact of being female – at work, in their social, sexual and moral choices.

The majority of the female population had now been made aware through what they watched and read for entertainment that they did not have to break down barriers to go out to work or choose not to have children. Popular culture had showed them what spending power could do to improve their lives, even though they still expected to live within the confines of home and family.

This vision of what was possible included their relationships with men and children. They could buy equipment to make housework easier and quicker; they could buy ready-made meals to take the chore out of cooking; they could buy time for themselves. Women's interests at this level coincided with men's to upset the old demarcations between the genders. This new unity of money-fuelled interests applied at a basic level among the mass of ordinary people. What brought them together to live a joined-up life was money, and the constant need for more of it. Magazines like this gave women the impression that they had no need to compete with men. They could have their cake and eat it without asking their permission.

Higher up the career ladder, where men now had to compete directly with overtly feminist women, old prejudices were just as strong as they had ever been. And so was the resentment. But here popular culture had no central role to play. Industrial tribunals and the sex equality laws were a more likely denouement.

The women's magazines also expanded popular culture into areas not previously used for propaganda statements, such as fashion and health. That these are now significant elements of female politics is due to pressure created through popular culture, rather than mainstream politics.

In doing so popular culture here also gives a quasi-political platform to role models it created. Mass-market magazine interviews solicited personal political comment, from feminist actresses like Emma Thompson to Page Three girl Sam Fox and even The Spice Girls. None of them, as the women they would have been without popular-culture celebrity, would have been likely to be in a position to make themselves heard, let alone be taken seriously as social arbiters. Consider how much greater was Glenda Jackson's impact on the mass of women through popular-culture outlets in films and on TV, and in newspaper and magazine interviews, than it was once she abandoned acting to become a Member of Parliament. Then her political expertise was revealed, like popular culture itself, as an ineffectual tool in a real-world context.

This tells us something important about the way popular culture works as a vehicle for political issues. To win support Jackson had first to be recognised as a celebrity and then *liked* by the mass of women as the person she projected on-screen or in magazines. People knew who she was, or they thought they did. She was able to express her political opinions publicly because as a celebrity women thought they knew and liked her. It was the process of popular culture which led them to think any such thing. It was as a notional persona created in women's minds that she was able to assume real political status. The emotions of the women she personified on film and television and what she said as herself in the House of Commons may have been equally passionately felt, but as a popular-culture star she had a direct route to the gut reaction. This did not carry through to reality. There was no mass judgement of the substance of what she said as long as people identified with her as a celebrity. They agreed with her if they liked her; they disagreed if they didn't. In the House people responded to what she said with their intellects, not their emotions, and were far less impressed.

A number of real women who gained power and influence from their celebrity status as popular-culture 'stars' became in public perception a kind of significant metaphor for ordinary women: As the medium they were the message, in a Marshall McLuhan sense. Pat Phoenix/Elsie Tanner had this kind of symbiosis among ordinary women, as, perhaps, did Helen Mirren/Jane Tennison for many. Joanna Lumley as Avenger Purdey, too. They then became important role models in both their inspirational popular-culture personae, and in the real-life identity women in general created for them. This is one example of something we will come back to later – how the distinctions between reality and fiction merge in the relationship between viewer/listener/reader and what they are given to see or hear.

The mass-market newspapers and magazines used popular culture's role models in this way to politicise ordinary women.

In effect these media appeared to bridge the cultural gap between the intellectual feminists and the ordinary woman. New women columnists, for example, moved away from home-bound navel-gazing at the kitchen sink to become the first quasi-rational female voices commenting on the altering state of the mass of women in society. The shift can be clearly seen by comparing the difference between Katharine Whitehorn's columns in the *Observer* and Julie Burchill's early work for the *Sunday Times*. Whitehorn was always affectionate and sympathetic towards women, whereas Burchill often seemed actually prepared to dislike some women, even despise them. She certainly came out with some objective criticisms of the female sex, Sacred Cows, she called them. For a woman from the ranks of the ordinary to criticise other women directly like this was probably the first public indication in popular culture that the female sex as a whole might be emerging as a political power group which might need to be taken seriously.

7

Popular culture might have changed women's demands and expectations, but it had not yet given them the means to bridge the traditional division between the sexes which had always blocked women's access to real political power.

Access to money did that. Once young women had spending power, that division began to crumble as men's time-honoured means of dominating women weakened. The differences between the genders then tended to be in women's minds. And there popular culture came into play.

For centuries women scarcely questioned an arbitrary gender division in society which divided women's lives and potential from men's. Simply, gender controlled function. Popular culture, in politicising the mass of women from inside the feminine ghetto, showed older women that their daughters at least could demand more interesting and fulfilled lives than their own; and it showed young women that the traditional path of wife and mother was as boring in real life as television soaps told them it was. They wanted to live like the women they saw and read about in the popular media. They wanted for themselves, in their own lives, the same stimulus as *Coronation Street* producer Bill Podmore had been looking for in soap opera – drama and a broad spectrum of emotional experience. Never mind if it was superficial.

Popular culture started to focus on youth. And then youth was female; young men splurged on their feminine side, in the way they dressed and wore their hair, and in a significant element of androgyny among pop idols and other media celebrities. Where they led, the young men on the street followed. In all its forms, popular culture had begun to concentrate on the growing importance of young women as a political entity.

As always, the political context the media in general created for these women was commercial.

Young women were no longer youthful versions of their mothers as those mothers had been of theirs. In the Fifties, fashion, for instance, did not differentiate between young and old. Women wore the same clothes, shoes, hairstyles, and bought the same furniture whatever their ages.

Attitudes like these had limited the commercial market, but, come the Sixties and Seventies, popular culture was having none of it. In magazines, in music, and on television, the media depended for growth on being able to persuade young women that the key to the lifestyle they wanted for themselves was a new, different image. An image dissociated as far as possible from any connection with older women's concept of femininity. Young women who had been released from traditional assumptions about themselves to expect more out of life than domesticity were looking en masse for new ways to define themselves in society. They were seeking a new identity.

These young women weren't waiting at home to get married. They went out to work; they earned money; they went shopping. Money gave them access to an ever-widening vista of popular culture – pop music, fashion, advertising, appearance – and they spent, spent, spent on the things popular culture was telling them they needed to live the dream. Their spending grew in economic importance.

The image they created for themselves – or rather, the image they adopted from the range offered by the popular culture of the day – gave them that 'personal' identity.

Embracing the images and standards of commercial popular culture embodied the young women's rebellion against compliance with the old order; popular culture *was* the rebellion. It gave the young a context for their redefinition of femininity; and they were the first generation who did not have to feel diminished by their gender and the way they wanted to use it outside the home.

These young women were also prepared to explore and experiment with sensual sensations, and their own emotions. This fed the market for popular culture with its focus on drama and extremes of feeling. Older women had suppressed their own feelings within the social framework of home, family and close community. The new sensation-seeking younger generation abandoned all such restraint in order to explore themselves. Their physicality became part of the way they expressed their emotions. Almost everything that was important to them was evinced in the way they looked, the way they sounded, and their sexual messages; the imperative was to look, sound, *be* young. Youth was an exclusive club, and an elitist one. Sexism, lookism, ageism, became part of common parlance, all geared to exclude anyone outside the pale of popular culture's definition of the new bright young things. The young women represented by popular culture at this time could be cruel in the way they repudiated older women's longing to belong to the club – as in the Nutrisse hair-colourant ad where Davina McCall's 'mother' says wistfully, 'Will it cover my few greys, dear?' and she says with malicious glee, '*All* your greys, mother.' As in 'You're old. Try to hide it, but you're old.'

Older generations might want to participate in popular culture's addiction to youth, but, like superannuated footballers, they could only sit and watch from the sidelines. As long as the world was presented and represented to them by the young and beautiful, they might feel they shared a kind of participation in the image by virtue of being women. But they couldn't belong; theirs was a different world. That was the theory, anyway.

Youth and sexual attraction appeared to be all young women needed to superimpose their images on the rest of society. Partly they could do this because of their unprecedented sexual freedom. Access to the contraceptive pill, freely available to single women from the late Sixties, had released sex from the backyard of the marital home and let it loose on the streets. Sex was no longer restricted to marriage. It did not even have to be synonymous with love. It was purely for pleasure, not an aspect of the social framework of society as it had been for the previous generation of ordinary women. It was part of entertainment, a by-product of a commercial industry involved in fashion, design, food, drink, beauty, advertising, and media manipulation.

Sex brought with it no responsibilities, no social ties. Young women could sleep with anyone they liked, someone different every night, someone whose name they didn't even know. Most of these young women probably expected one day to marry and have children, but not yet. They wanted to explore themselves, their own feelings and attitudes, they wanted all the excitement and pleasure and sensation that popular culture was offering them. They wanted to be aware that they were having the time of their lives. Sex was a kind of measure of that, a currency for new popular-culture commercial expansion in advertising, photography, newspapers and magazines, on television, and in popular fiction, too. Once 'society' impinged on the euphoria of the young it would all be over.

At the time, this seemed a part of the natural process of living. These women felt safe to try to ignore society beyond their own youth because popular culture told them that there were no wider consequences to what they were doing.

Being young seemed risk-free. If they got pregnant outside marriage, their mothers might still try to make them marry the father and bring up the baby, parents were old, they would say that, wouldn't they? These new young women had other options.

After 1967, they could have an abortion; or they could have the child adopted. If they caught a sexually transmitted disease? Take a pill. There was a pill for most bad things. If they were too fat, there was a pill for it. That this contained a live tapeworm was neither here nor there: *il faut souffrir pour être belle*. There were pills for worms, too. There were pills to overcome inhibitions or exhaustion, pills to make you happy, pills to calm you down, even pills that offered a euphoric view of other people. *Love is in the Air* went the song and it felt like it was true. Young women wanted to feel invincible, and they were as long as they looked and acted as though they were. Popular culture didn't tell them any different, the world was full of love, and they were part of it. As long as they looked and sounded and acted as popular culture prescribed, they were loved. And that was what they wanted.

There was nothing then to stop the young. Popular culture had cleared the path for their self-indulgence with those early films which had questioned the old-fashioned tenets of respectability, the idea that losing your virginity could ruin your future. Now any remaining moral scruples were swept away by the opinion-forming media. Faint-hearted morality didn't sell; there was no money in holding back. Sex did sell, and it sold everything, from fashion to cars.

A few protested at the moral chaos of the sexual free-for-all. But popular culture's publicity machine, the media, soon disposed of kill-joys like Mary Whitehouse. The feminists, too, disliked what they saw as the exploitation of women's sexuality. At one point they even started to detect messages of subliminal exploitation in advertisements, convinced that they could see the word sex 'hidden' in photographs of almost everything from perfume bottles to toasters in ads in magazines, on television and videos, or along the sides of London Transport buses.

Such voices urging caution were incidental. Young women were intoxicated with their own sudden importance as popular culture consumers. They were calling the tune, and this had never happened to women before, or not since Boadicea, anyway, long before living memory, and no one was interested in emotional ancient history, only in today.

This was a far cry from these young women's mothers, who earlier had been made constantly aware by earlier popular culture that though they could dream, their function as women was to care for others. The popular culture of their day had reflected that on TV and radio where women were in their element counselling distressed friends or troubled children, in talking through problems and providing shoulders to cry on; and in advertisements like the Oxo campaign featuring the mumsy Katie; and in series centred on mums as centre of the family, like Doris in the early episodes of *The Archers* or *EastEnders'* Lou Beale.

Now young women were a new, self-absorbed generation, encouraged to put their own feelings first even if they were careless of the consequences of their actions on others. Popular culture encouraged this. It set about creating a groundswell of emotional concentration on self which characterised a majority of young women then. Where older women had been given a glimpse of a wider world through the television, radio, magazines and books within their own domestic settings, popular culture was pushing the young away from the home and out to the bright lights of city streets to act out all the sensations and indulgences available on the market.

The older women, however much they yearned to expand the arena of their lives beyond home and family, had nevertheless always expected from childhood that one day their prince would come and they would live happily ever after. Once a year, perhaps, they could get a taste of what might have been in an exotic dream location with one of the new cheap package tours. For the young, though, popular culture was making nonsense of the whole concept of happily every after. They wanted to be happy now, this minute.

Whether we like it or not, we are all defined by our age in terms of our attitudes and our beliefs. This new generation of young women had, from the time they were children, been losing connection with the domestic realities of their housebound mothers' lives. They simply were not interested in the skills once assumed as part of femininity – keeping house, for want of another word. Caring for others, cooking, cleaning, changing the beds, were what mothers did, not New Women. Nor was popular culture interested in involving them in any kind of notional preparation for the lives they would have to adapt to once they were no longer part of youth, no longer special, but part of society in general; there was no profit in that. The mass media concentrated on providing an entirely different context for young women's lives; it focused on life in the city centre and metropolitan areas where popular culture lived on the street. It distanced the young from their mothers' generation. Older women's image was wrong. Too often they were embarrassing in their efforts to reinvent some kind of communication with their children, trying to hold on to a connection. Many tried to discard the mothering role to masquerade as sisters or friends, which could only further alienate them from younger women for whom the appeal of youth culture was that it had nothing to do with dreary realities like ageing.

The young, though, no longer saw the family as the centre of their lives. Put in front of television screens while their mothers tried to catch up with the housework when they returned from work, children had moved away from parental influence to connect instead with their friends at school, and the mass culture they had in common. In the evenings, they hid out in their own rooms to play records or read magazines like *Honey* which were targeted at their age group. They watched teenagers like themselves in *Hollyoaks* or *Neighbours* or *Grange Hill*, and through the media they became part of self-functioning peer groups, where kids have a kind of independent contiguous existence outside the adult world in which parents and teachers seem to have little knowledge of, or relevance to, the realities of their children's lives.

In the media it is always the children who are a priority both to themselves and to adults. They are judged by their peer groups, and they judge others by those same standards set by their popular culture. In particular music, and musicians, define their emotional lives, providing them with a separate street life adults cannot share. And that separation is crucial to the appeal of the forms of media which express the way they feel and what they want.

This applies to every one of popular culture's generations. It is true, too, of women who lived particularly intensely before the advent of the mass media – times of war, for example. With hindsight there is a discernible shift from a more traditional, if grudging, acceptance of a female, domestic role in hit songs like Tammy Wynette's *Stand By Your Man* or Helen Reddy's *I Am Woman* or Gloria Gaynor's *I Will Survive,* compared with the anthems of the emotionally self-absorbed, free-spirited younger women like Whitney Houston's version of *I'm Every Woman,* or Duffy's . . . *To Survive, I've Got To Be Alive, I've Got To Be Me.*

Where the older generation still saw themselves as part of society as a whole, the younger belonged only to an age group which filled their own world. They simply cut off from the rest.

These young women went out to work and the jobs they did were often associated with popular culture's 'image' industries like fashion, interior design, public relations; they earned money; they went shopping for cheap clothes they could throw away rather than wash. Money gave them access to an ever-widening vista of popular culture – pop music, fashion, advertising, and sex as a tool to open the doors of sensually charged leisure. Popular culture was telling them what they needed to live the dream, and they went out and bought it.

One effect of this was that all aspects of popular culture

merged to become a single entity. Television, magazines, music and the rest were no longer discrete aspects of mass culture, they interacted as a single, interdependent industry, the media. English *Vogue* spoke for popular culture as a whole when it said at the time, 'Fashion is self-consciously sociological and frankly feather-brained. It's classic and immediate. Nostalgic and now. Worldly and other-worldly. Whatever's happening, you are part of it, and at last you can be yourself and look as you choose.'

The mass of young women did not care what was happening to society in general; only that something was happening to them. Popular culture offered a lifestyle blueprint for younger women who were not motivated to change their traditional mindset, because they were not aware of having one. They wanted to become the women whose images popular culture created to inspire them. Advertisements showed them what they should look like, how they should make up, what clothes they should wear, all to look 'fabulous'. The word is significant. They wanted to look unreal, and as unlike their ordinary selves as possible. And because the nature of popular culture is facile and irrational and undemanding, they swallowed whole the simplistic message that popular culture itself gave them the means to be anything they wanted. All that was necessary was to get the image right. Watch celebrities, read about them, look like them and speak like them, and no one would know the difference.

To the media entrepreneurs still existing in the real world, this was a commercial opportunity not to be missed. Some became celebrities in their own right, projecting a fairy-godmother image of their own as popular culture creates its own enablers. Record producers like Pete Waterman and

Simon Cowell became much more important than their celebrity products because they gave ordinary young women the chance to live the dream.

Popular culture now tells us that the performer is the product and the criterion for selling the product is certainly not talent, or even ability, it is 'star quality'. That is the factor which projects an image which connects with the aspirations of each new wave of popular culture's consumers.

And don't doubt that it is the entrepreneurs of popular culture who tailor this quality for the market. And it's nothing new. It becomes only too obvious when 'stars' disconnect themselves from their producers to go it alone. The celebrity careers of Helen Reddy or Petula Clark never survived rifts with husbands who were their managers.

Commercial elements have forced popular culture to alter its approach to this new affluent young market. Previously the business interests behind popular culture had tended to use the media to tell women what they didn't know they wanted; now those interests had to listen to these young women and to provide what they demanded. Young women knew exactly what they wanted, and popular culture had become their only means of getting it.

This was the source of their political importance. It was based on their spending power, and also on their significance as a very large, discrete group. Society outside that group tended to indulge them in the assumption that these were the people on whom the social framework of the country would depend in future. Except that popular culture images and attitudes which shaped them gave them no sense of social responsibility, and no real concept of what the future must involve.

Neither the older generation of women nor the commercial

entrepreneurs behind popular culture understood these young women. The entrepreneurs only knew what sold. They did not understand that the preoccupations of young people with sex and money were not simply an abnegation of a sense of duty towards the population as a whole, a refusal to accept personal responsibility for anyone or anything. They were also a denial of what everyone outside the charmed group defined as real life.

Young women didn't want real life. They saw their mothers' dissatisfaction as real life, and they refused to accept it. They wanted the illusion of something much better which was what popular culture delivered. They wanted to belong to a kind of sentimental conglomerate of like-minded – or, rather, like-feeling – young women, and, as long as they conformed to popular culture's stereo-typical images, they participated in that illusion.

There was nothing to make young women question their own self-interest. Popular culture had provided them with political power as consumers; now it had released them from a sense of social duty, and introduced them to the concept of entitlement. A whole generation of young women were sold on the conviction that, because government policy reflected their interests as spenders, they were entitled to anything they wanted. 'I'm entitled' replaced the old feminist mantra 'It's not fair'.

Of course those image-conscious, self-indulgent, un-realistic and gloriously unrestricted young women had moments of doubt. But those doubts tended to be about themselves and their own status within the framework of belonging laid down by popular culture. They were worried about what they looked like, how their peers perceived them, why they were depressed because they did not feel themselves fulfilled. In part, this is the way popular culture still works. Many cannot get off the roller-coaster; they have to go further, into addiction or eating disorders or self-harm.

Inevitably a world view based on self-image and illusion has casualties. Popular culture always gives people reason to believe that they belong. What they belong to, though, is a huge group of ordinary people who have been brainwashed into a mindset where intellect and powers of reason are perceived actually to counteract popular culture's effortless illusory dreamworld. For these young women there is nothing real to belong to. There's a huge gulf between their irrational expectations and a reality which defines them as unskilled, unrealistic and often resentful. Popular culture laid the foundations for generations of dysfunctional women.

Nevertheless the economy now depended on these women and their spending power. There was no turning back the clock to take away or redirect their insubstantial political importance. Like Dr Frankenstein, popular culture had created a monster it could not control, only pacify. And like the nameless monster, these women, empowered by the crass, trivial and irrational diversions of the mass media, went on the rampage to destroy society's traditional values in a desperate search for a society which would understand and shelter them.

8

This is not a book about men and women; it's about different aspects of women and what happens when they gain the power to lay down criteria for the way other women live. However, since female power and influence involved the dissolution of an existing male-orientated system, there has to be some consideration, in discussing how popular culture empowered women and changed their lives, of the role played by men, and how the changes in women's attitudes affected them.

In the real world, the weight of numbers of the women who had been empowered by popular culture, and consequently transformed into consumers on a vast scale, gave them significant political authority. Women en masse had become a significant factor in the country's economic survival.

Men were slow to react to what was happening to women. The feminists they dismissed as peripheral extremists, but they failed to see that popular culture was liberating ordinary women from their dependence on father and husband within the confines of marriage, home and children.

Men on the whole failed to adapt to meet women's changing demands and their abiding need for the sense of security which men had traditionally provided. They became defensive, not understanding that the women popular culture was empowering were seeking self-expression and recognition of their needs within the established male-orientated system. They still looked to that system, and to men, for protection and support. Popular culture understood this need.

The media took care to provide women at least with the illusion of being secure and protected. So, as previously mentioned, gentlemanly elderly newsreaders like Robert Dougall and Sandy Gall managed to make them feel shielded from harm regardless of what was going on in the world; the policemen in *Dixon of Dock Green* and *Z-Cars* kept the streets safe, and provided a notional shoulder to cry on when the real world was too intrusive; and *Emergency Ward Ten* and *Dr Kildare* were there to comfort the unhappy and heal suffering. Popular culture at least gave the impression that the male world still existed as a sort of back-up if things went wrong. But popular culture's masculine figures were not the real-world men that ordinary women were used to. These were sensitive and caring men who combined understanding with the ability to act. To quote the old-fashioned bastion of male supremacy, Dr Gillespie in *Dr Kildare*, 'Our job is to keep people alive, not to tell them how to live their lives.' Dr Gillespie represented reality, but, when Dr Kildare invariably let his finer feelings get the better of him and ignored his boss to break the rules, few women did not think the better of him for it.

Of course, popular culture's semblance of quasi-masculine protection was only notional, but it still gave women a new confidence to test-drive new attitudes and needs.

The protective aspect of popular culture's role in ordinary women's lives depended on its ability to make them feel good about themselves. Phrases like 'retail therapy', 'shopaholic' and 'chocaholic' entered the language to describe the comforting aspects of the self-indulgences available. Women were empowered on an individual level to spoil themselves – 'You Know You're Worth It', a popular advertising slogan told them. They felt that popular culture was speaking directly to them, and therefore they were important. No one asked them to justify that assumption.

Women didn't have to ask what made them important. They knew the answer. Once they would have said as wives and mothers, as carers or home-makers. Now they knew that they were important in their own right. And they were the first generation of ordinary women who could say that. Popular culture had helped them to boost their own self-esteem.

This new confidence was fuelled by the commercial opportunities which made this mass of female consumers important to all forms of the media and commerce. History and long practice were not easily overturned. For centuries women had scarcely questioned an arbitrary gender division in society which divided women's lives and potential from men's. Simply, they had accepted that gender controlled their function. Now popular culture was telling them that gender was immaterial, they could define their own function.

Coincidentally, at the same time as women were being empowered to be more assertive about what they wanted for themselves, and to hell with all those princes who failed to turn up, it was men's traditional bastions of power which were under attack. Men were being marginalised in society as a whole. As women began to see themselves as separate from the established preconceptions about women's place in society, and no longer an autonomous part of a hier-archical male-dominated social structure, it was popular culture that filled the vacuum left by men's loss of their own traditional role within a male-orientated social system.

The concept of the male as hunter-gatherer was in

transition. Women's contribution to the family budget was now often vital for survival, not simply useful. Women's perception of men in the old macho-style male hierarchical social setup was crumbling too. The demands of popular culture for extreme emotion, which gave proxy involvement with others to millions of women, meant that traditional he-men were of limited interest. Theirs was not a role which fitted the new female preference for sympathetic, emotional men who featured in TV soaps or the happy endings of romantic fiction. He-men were constricted in their emotional range and they undervalued women. It was a new, softer-edged kind of male to whom women responded on the screen, in advertising, in popular songs.

The concept of the caring, listening lover was a new market to exploit for the female consumer, and popular culture simply adjusted the image of men to meet demand. There was no overt intention to operate outside the male system; it was possible for men and women to cohabit within that established setup. But the masculine, hierarchical order on which society had been based for centuries may well have been shaken by women's new political empowerment and the terms by which popular culture had achieved this. For a start, men had had to change their perception of what femininity entailed.

The early seminal soaps and sitcoms were made by men, and as far as these men were concerned the women in them had to be driven to emotional extremes because real women's lives as wives and mothers were too boring to interest mass audiences. That in itself suggests that popular culture did force a change in men's perception of women. It would have been the sudden revelation of hidden female passions that surprised men; most of them expected their wives' lives to be boring. Now they were presented with a rather different image of themselves in relation to women.

Humorous columns in the newspapers, from Colin Reid (*Daily Mail*) in the 1960s to Martyn Harris (*Daily Telegraph*) in the 80s and New Men like David Thomas in the 90s reflected changes in men's perception of their role in the family and society. The male becomes progressively more peripheral and put upon by women. In the *Weekend Guardian* of 2008, Tim Dowling presents himself as having about as much status within his family as the dog, which, as far as I know, doesn't even have a name.

But surely this is all tongue in cheek. It should not be taken as a serious male concession to the power of the female. It isn't. What it does hint at is a growing under-current of antagonism towards women which men think it worth their while to keep to themselves. It suggests that men have started not to feel at home with the female sex.

Men made no move to stop popular culture from becoming a vehicle for women to achieve independence, and hence political power. That's because on the whole those men despised its intellectual and moral content. They did not take it seriously. They have never understood the terms of reference, the powerful symbolism of emotion. Or the nature of the power base they inadvertently provided for women, the community of the mass consumer.

When it was already too late, men tried to use popular culture to redress the balance. They flocked to see Michael Douglas in the film *Wall Street* with its message that Greed is Good, and that the ruthless man prevails. This message didn't work as a ploy to impress women as it did for men because the dominant male in the movie justifies his actions intellectually. His inability to feel anything outside the power surge of successful acquisition cuts him off from the inevitably emotional and sentimental reactions of women. His relationships with women, too, were often akin to takeover deals.

Popular culture took the feminine view. Male pre-dilections and priorities in all their absurdity were ridiculed in TV shows like *Men Behaving Badly* and *Cheers*, or in popular songs like Carly Simon's *'You're So Vain, I Betcha Think This Song Is About You'*. The mass media presented men as ersatz infants, an entire gender reduced in women's lives to the nursery school.

Men didn't seem to understand what was happening to them. In 1990, Robert Bly's huge bestseller, *Iron John*, set out to counter women's demands that men should get in touch with their feminine side. If they did, he said, they lost their means of survival as men. *Iron John* argues that men should get in touch with their essential maleness, their basic role as hunters, and go down to the woods and bang drums and bond. Bly's book was a tacit warning to men that unless they fought back, women would destroy their innate masculinity. And this message was driven home in the mass media, where the shifting images of male identity crises were mirrored by hermaphrodite rock bands and female-triumphalist lyrics of popular songs from girl groups.

Iron John was part of men's attempts to show that the reality of gender equality is a pernicious myth, and that popular culture's attempts to prove otherwise have caused individual unhappiness and social breakdown since it became a fact of women's lives.

But it was a last-ditch attempt to hold back the tide of Girl Power throughout popular culture.

For all the talk there has been for the last four decades

about the Sex War and gender inequality – called 'the Saigon of the Sex War' in the 1960s – the real issue between men and women is about men and women's fluctuating economic power. Historically, that's what men had, and women did not. That is where men have lost their dominance since the 1990s.

Loss of economic dominance has marginalised men in society as a whole. Women's economic clout as consumers has for the first time given them a defining role in influencing almost all the political policies which shape our social system now.

For which, ironically, they have to thank Margaret Thatcher.

This is ironic because the Iron Lady made no effort to disguise an apparent lack of any interest at all in other women, and certainly not in what they had to say. Feminists loathed her for this very reason, protesting that, as one of very few women with real power, she did not use it to help other women to become achievers. Margaret Thatcher ignored their criticism that she was not a real woman; that she was a man in woman's clothing; even unnatural. She did not bother to argue, as did Barbara Castle (a politician much admired by feminists), that she had succeeded in a man's world with no particular advantages, and if she could do it, so could others, so let them do as she had done without any help from her. Mrs Thatcher simply did not react to the abuse she got from feminists. She ignored them.

The Thatcher phenomenon had a lot to do with popular culture's empowerment of the mass of ordinary women. The really galling thing about her, even to mild feminists, was always that she was quintessentially one of the ranks of ordinary women, and remained so in spite of the power she achieved. She had no overt intention of overturning the masculine system, which she accepted as a support structure which it was assumed most women found comforting, even liberating.

She knew that her real constituency was among ordinary women, practical women who had no time for artistic or intellectual flannel when they had a family to care for. There's no surprise at all that Margaret Thatcher made her defining political statement 'There is no such thing as society', not to the *Economist* or the *Financial Times*, but to Douglas Keays, an interviewer from *Woman's Own*. This was a middle-of-the-road magazine which, in spite of revamps, still catered for the more conservative of popular culture's converts, married women with a growing family, ordinary women who were interested primarily in home, domestic expertise and family life. Margaret Thatcher knew where her support lay.

But Thatcher wasn't addressing her female audience simply as women like herself; she was interested in them as a constituency of voters who felt close to her because they understood what she was saying. She knew exactly what it was like to be a woman feeling helpless as everything that she saw as familiar female territory – husband, children, family and friends – was swept away by the pace of social change. She wanted to revive the traditional female common sense and family-based values which she thought had made Victorian Britain a force to be reckoned with in the world. At the same time she alienated many women who were not feminists because, as quintessential ordinary woman, she reminded them how much they disliked certain aspects of their own femininity.

Which adds to the irony that in trying to restore the framework of masculine-dominated family values, Thatcher destroyed the established male social system. She did what the feminists failed to do; she turned government of the country feminine.

Popular culture had a lot to do with the Margaret Thatcher method of government. This in spite of the fact that she was brought up in a strict church-going household where leisure activities were expected to improve the shining hour. There is no evidence that she was prevented from accessing popular culture because it was frivolous, but she was serious-minded and hard-working so she may have found the sensuality of almost all its aspects quite daunting. Even so, she was not intellectual, and it was on the basis of feminine intuition that she understood the importance of image and playing to people's emotions which made popular culture so powerful.

As a politician she personified ordinary women. She was the daughter of a small shopkeeper and his wife who brought up their daughter to respect a woman's role as wife, mother, and her husband's helpmeet. She entered politics under the financial protection of a supportive breadwinner husband; she took pride in running the country's economy as though it was the household accounts. She made important decisions – like investment in the railways – on the basis of personal prejudice. Sir Peter Parker, then chairman of British Rail, told a story he'd heard to explain her adamant refusal to subsidise the system, that Mrs T. had suffered an incident on a train along the lines of Aunt Ada Doom in *Cold Comfort Farm* 'seeing something nasty in the woodshed', and ever afterwards felt a personal hatred for trains. Mythical or not, her decisions on the subject were undoubtedly based on emotion, not reason.

In office, she made no attempt to disguise the fact that she chose her henchmen in true popular-culture style on the basis of their looks or their admiration for her. She dominated them like an ageing diva with her toyboys. We probably shouldn't be surprised when the Cabinet ministers she chose on this basis began to act like soap stars living out a melodramatic script, and several had to resign. Cecil Parkinson, David Mellor, Jeffrey Archer, Neil Hamilton . . . It must be significant that several of them then actually turned to popular culture as celebrities to make a living.

Thatcher surrounded herself with yes-men and she fairly shamelessly flaunted her femininity to charm old-fashioned macho international supremos like Ronald Reagan and President Mitterand into submission.

Popular culture, for which in this case we can read the mass media, loved her. If the quality papers didn't, because she was illiberal, anti-intellectual, and rigidly right wing, they loved to hate her. She was a figure the media would have had to invent as a metaphor for a dominating mother figure if she hadn't existed already in an even more extreme form than her *Spitting Image* persona. An entire electorate, whatever their political opinions, regressed to toddler-hood in the face of her Mother Knows Best approach to government. Either they bowed to Mother's authority, or they threw tantrums in defiance.

As Prime Minister, putting her house in order for her extended family of voters, she trampled the established male hierarchical social systems like cockroaches. This did not happen because of any deliberate policy decision to do so.

Given the devastating unemployment and industrial decline during her period in power, it came naturally to her to cut back to balance the books. In this case, this involved huge male unemployment.

As part of the cleaning-up process, she set out to break one of the strongest residues of male bonding, the trades unions. In doing so, she systematically reduced the country's manufacturing base, cutting the output of this predominantly male arena by 30 per cent between 1979 and 1983. Skilled and unskilled men in the shipbuilding, coal, and steel industries lost their jobs, and with it their status within the family and in society as a whole.

To make up the gap in men's capacity to spend, Thatcher recognised the market opportunities that arose in response to demand from women with buying power. She increased that economic power. She created hundreds of thousands of 'women's' jobs in the service and caring industries. To men, these were not real jobs; many were temporary, or part-time, to fit in with women's family commitments. It was a Thatcher priority to preserve conservative attitudes about women's role in society. The growth in these female-orientated industries, which also began to depend heavily on the growth in new computer technology which was largely operated, even if not designed, by women, helped the country recover from a serious economic recession.

But men's status was degraded. Desperate workers in heavy industries which had relied on their strength as well as their skills, in shipbuilding and the steel industries among others, were told to retrain to get work. One displaced shipyard worker, a riveter, was advised to take up knitting as an alternative way to earn a living. Thatcher's bracing attitudes to men's hopelessness appeared to many as if the government acted as though they had brought disaster on themselves simply by being male.

No one seemed to notice the extent to which men's status was being eroded, or how thoroughly the hierarchical systems on which the male sex had always based its dominance were being demolished.

More devastating still, once they were destroyed there was nothing else in their lives to take the place of these old bastions of male power. Margaret Thatcher left men with nothing to take pride in. This applied at a very basic individual level, within marriage, and the family, as well as in the wider arena of work and government.

No one seemed to understand the implications of men losing their self-respect. Thatcher managed to make the mass of ordinary working men question their own function in society as they had never done before. They saw themselves as being humiliated; they were angry but helpless. Nor did they see what was happening in terms of the political necessity of economic crisis. They blamed Mrs Thatcher on a very personal level.

Their own futile resentment made the situation worse for men, who saw themselves humiliated by the wiles of a despised female rather than by the mere incompetence of other men. Perhaps to an extent they were right; no group of men dealing with the political crises of the time would have acted so ruthlessly to disable their own sex.

As far as men were concerned, Margaret Thatcher was a perfectly ordinary woman; she was neither brilliant nor charismatic nor glamorous. She looked like a housewife; she dressed like a housewife; she addressed the House of Commons like the president of a local Townswomen's Guild speaking to a meeting; she was a dedicated wife and a mother. When she started on her career, she seemed to treat politics as part of a housewife's day, like voluntary work. These displaced men had seen her elected by a considerable proportion of female voters like herself; to them she stood for all women, ergo women were responsible for and approved the annihilation of the male. From this point, men began to distrust ordinary women. That may now be masked because men are marginalised in so many aspects of everyday life, but their distrust has not diminished, and they have not adjusted to a feminised version of a social system they had once taken for granted was dominated by male values and priorities.

9

In one sense, ordinary women gained from the virtual destruction of British manufacturing industry. In the new service and care industries which Thatcher created to kickstart the ravaged economy, women started out with a definite advantage, which was not the case in the heavy industries. Newly empowered by popular culture, they did not have to compete with men for a place in the new workforce, and any lack of formal skills did not hamper them. This was their traditional domain. Manufacturing industry had demanded physical strength, where women could not often equal men. But the service industries, demanding administrative skills, dexterity to operate computers, or dealing with people, seemed little more than an extension of women's formerly unpaid domestic skills.

Mrs Thatcher had told *Woman's Own* 'There's no such thing as society.' She meant that individuals were ultimately responsible for their own and their families' lives. In her farewell speech in the House of Commons she said, 'We have given back control to the people over their own lives and over their livelihoods, over the decisions that matter most to them and their families . . . ' What she had done for women was give them the capability to do what her mother had done for her father in the grocery shop in Grantham; she gave women in their own families control of the purse strings. In short, Margaret Thatcher was the iconic house-wife and mother of pre-popular culture, running the country exactly as she would administer the household budget, or the grocery shop she might well have taken over from her father had she not become Prime Minister.

In the context of the State, her message to millions of other women like herself was to bring up their families to stand on their own two feet, and to defend home and hearth against interfering busybodies. In terms of government, those interfering busybodies were statutory authority and bureaucracy, and as Prime Minister she rolled back the frontiers of state intervention in people's personal lives.

But actually, she left behind a floundering social system based on an obsolete framework of distorted male-orientated institutions and practices. She created a power vacuum for women to fill, but she did not provide any kind of support system which could show them how to do it. When it came down to the wire, she was not able to do it herself when her own support system failed and she was thrown out.

Among the ruins, only popular culture now seemed to express and embody the ambitions and expertise of the women who were keeping the economy going. Adherence to the principles of mass culture – its greed, its cult of self, its dependence for effect on the lowest common denominator – had reduced the scope of political ideas and ethical concepts to a wallowing state of mass feeling. John Major's premiership as Margaret Thatcher's successor only underlined how ineffectual the male establishment had become. What Thatcher left behind was a dysfunctional government.

It was, though, a feminised government. This does not mean that Parliament was suddenly filled with women Members of Parliament. Feminisation in this sense meant that women were the economic mainstay of the workforce, and they tended as a consequence to set the agenda within the family. This manifested itself in terms of government in the growing influence of women's concerns and in pressure for instant emotionally satisfying solutions to social problems rather than interest in strategy and planning. The right-to-buy policy over council housing is a case in point, where no thought was given to what would replace the social housing stock. Feminised government is short-termist government.

Margaret Thatcher may have given women the chance to dominate our political and social life for years to come, but she gave this to ordinary women, the women empowered by popular culture, not to feminists or highly qualified or intellectual women. In effect, she allowed popular culture to manipulate political power in the land.

Margaret Thatcher did not create Dr Christine de Panafieu's vital change-agent women. She was not out to effect fundamental social change. It was to ordinary women that she gave a united voice, but it was not an independent voice. Ordinary women were not broken of their habit of looking for support and guidance. They knew nothing else.

There was a psychological chasm opening up between the sexes. Men had lost the source of their pride in themselves. They had nowhere to exercise the competitive aspects of their nature common to all male animals. Being reduced to competing against women as breadwinners and even as father-figures to their children was a humiliation too far for many. They blamed women for what they saw as some kind of sneaky coup.

A few men became 'New Men' or house-husbands, and tried to take on the woman's traditional domestic role. But though the woman's role had been perceived for centuries as subordinate to men's, men soon learned that it involved skills and abilities of a high order in themselves. Failure to equal their wives' achievements at home could further lower their self-esteem. Nor did their female partners always accept giving up a share of their role to men; they found it hard to give up domestic control, particularly where this involved decisions about the children – what immunisations they should have, where they should go to school.

At the same time, men had to stand aside and watch as women proved they could fulfil a man's role in the family and at work. They resented the automatic female expectation that she was entitled to retain her dominance in the traditional maternal and domestic role. Men increasingly played a marginal role in their own lives. And women, too, were becoming aware of this. They were learning that men need not be central to living their lives, not as breadwinners, not as husbands, nor as fathers.

I remember, when I was writing a weekly column called 'Workface' for the *Guardian* women's page in the Eighties, interviewing a middle-aged man who had just lost his executive job in public relations. He was married, with two pre-teenage children, and he was very worried about keeping his family afloat. As we talked he became very distressed.

'I don't know how I'm going to get another job,' he said. 'I go to an interview and they ask questions, but what can I tell them about myself? I don't know who I am any more. I used to introduce myself as John Smith of the company and that's who I was. Now I'm just John Smith. I don't feel I exist as a person, so how can I expect anyone else to think I do?'

He was not alone. In those What Kind of Person Are You? personality quizzes popular in magazines, there's always an opening question along the lines of 'Who are you?' According to the people who compile these questionnaires, men invariably answer this by putting down the job they do or where they work. Women almost always say first that they are married, mothers, have blonde hair, or a bubbly personality.

The point is that the aftermath of Margaret Thatcher's economic and industrial policies dealt a body blow to male self-esteem and boosted women's. In their hundreds of thousands – there were three million unemployed – men floundered to retain some sort of masculine identity when the standards by which they set their own status in society as a whole had been demolished.

The arena where the feminisation of society and its institutions could make itself felt was popular culture, and this began to dictate that what were categorised as male characteristics – violence, aggression, insensitivity – were condemned by the mass media as anti-social. Even outright competition became politically incorrect. There were to be no losers, only runners up. Meritocracy was suspect and associated with privilege, ability seen as a form of being born with a silver spoon in your mouth. Popular culture precepts influenced attitudes to education: 'Be happy, not successful'; 'study to discover yourself, not to pass exams'.

It was more important for the weakest to do something however badly than for the strong to do it well. No one could fail, just taking part was a triumph. Popular culture was adapting women's old role as caring and supportive to the new female-orientated society. Television presented men as inadequate – *Cheers*, or *Friends*. Even Clark Kent came over as a bit of a jerk until he turned into Superman. Men let women down, in *Desperate Housewives*, for example; or they were women-chasers or rapists. In every magazine agony column, they featured heavily as love rats or being cruelly unwilling to commit.

Men's crisis of confidence got no sympathy from women. As a generalisation, women seemed to blame men for what was happening to the masculine ethos. A considerable proportion of ordinary women still looked to men to be strong for them. Many still preferred to go to a male doctor, accountant or lawyer. This had nothing to do with the quality of professional ability, though feminists thought it had. It was about ordinary women's innate assumption that a man would want to help her because she was a woman. They did not trust another woman in the same way.

We are not talking here about feminists; the women at issue were rather those who had been brought up within the male hierarchical system, and accepted this as a framework for their own lives. They had not sought and did not want the breakdown of the masculine structure which told them where they belonged in the scheme of things. Jealousy has always been recognised as a problem for women on a personal level, but they can also become possessive of their old-style femininity en masse. They are jealous of their status, however much the feminists despised it, and they close ranks against change. It was not men who reacted against women's breaking ranks in response to popular culture's opening up of their prospects, it was other women. All men were implicated in the failure of the traditional male hierarchies, and women felt betrayed.

True, women as a whole had no precedent for the general collapse of masculinity, which might have given them insight into how they could help. Instinct, born of long tradition, taught them to rally to the family good, to fill the gap left by the breakdown of the men's role, and if that meant forging ahead regardless, so be it. But they were not going to allow the men who had betrayed them to take for themselves their own victimhood. Simply, as a gender men lost political significance.

Men were in crisis, and unpractised in dealing with their resulting emotions. Here logic and reason were ineffectual. Women, well versed in feelings, had no idea what it felt like to be a man. They could not empathise. Popular culture had concentrated their empowerment in an overwhelmingly female way.

Divorce rates soared; suicide in young men increased; rather mysteriously, sperm counts fell. There was a strong undercurrent of male vindictiveness against women. Men grew more wary about becoming too involved with women; they were wary of being used. Newspapers started writing about a new trend among women to see their relationships as commercial propositions. Women, it seemed, were seducing men as an investment opportunity. The suburban madam Cynthia Payne's flourishing business entertaining men with sex in her Streatham terrace house says something about men's growing fear of the financial consequences of commitment. When Heidi Fleisch was prosecuted on a similar charge in Hollywood, people were astonished that famous male sex symbols from the film industry paid for her services when they could have had sex on demand for nothing. But they were protecting themselves against the women who might exploit the opportunity for blackmail or cry assault.

Women were also pursuing their own interests to dominate attitudes in the workplace. Their economic importance as consumers gave them considerable political clout. They used this – the form of mass empowerment that popular culture had given them – to make the social system female-friendly.

Popular culture came up with 'girl power', a phrase which was initially associated with several groups in the early 1990s – for example the indie band Helen Love and the pop-punk duo Shampoo – but became part of media language with The Spice Girls.

The *Oxford English Dictionary* defined 'Girl Power':

Power exercised by girls; specifically a self-reliant attitude among girls and young women manifested in ambition, assertiveness and individualism. Although also used more widely (especially as a slogan), the term has been particularly and repeatedly associated with popular music ... most notably in the late 1990s with the British all-female group The Spice Girls.

In the Nineties as the economy recovered and un-employment dropped, men went back to work to find the workplace quite changed. The old meritocracy they had operated was gone. Competitiveness directed against women was discouraged, and women's demands for flexible hours, child-friendly attitudes and protection against discrimination on the grounds of pregnancy were enshrined in law. Industrial tribunals dealt with a string of cases brought by women over real or imagined discrimination or sexual harassment. Meanwhile on television Alexis Colby in *Dynasty* and a series of tough and successful women (Connie Beauchamp in *Holby City*, Kim Tate in *Emmerdale*) regularly harassed men sexually without fear of retribution.

Many men lost confidence in their maleness, to the extent

that they could no longer trust their own judgement. If they did try to act upon it, their actions could perhaps be illegal.

In addition, men did not represent a potential commercial growth market in their own right, as women had when popular culture set out to exploit it. Sport was the one male area ripe for exploitation. Participants here – horses and football stars – are notoriously unpredictable; nor are the emotions they engender usually conducive to feelings which are, in popular-culture terms, socially appropriate as role models. Here commercial interests behind the mass market made efforts to exploit male xenophobia. Sporting encounters took on the intensity of war. Men rather pathetically asserted their identities by wearing team colours and singing club anthems.

Otherwise, popular culture had nothing much to gain from shifting its methods and attention specifically towards men. Ordinary women remained a much more rewarding focus for media attention.

10

Margaret Thatcher reduced and marginalised the importance of men's role in society; she also started a process in which it became accepted that government should be built on image rather than the traditional operation of political systems.

The image of women as a whole, in the media, on television, and in advertisements, as well as in the way government projected itself, became more aggressive. Popular culture no longer exclusively presented women in the old good and bad lights, where good women had to be likeable, and the unlikeable were bad. Margaret Thatcher presented government policy as a series of maternal precepts, but this was not happening only in the corridors of power. Popular culture was now depicting images of women as more assertive. On television, and in advertisements, for instance, women shown in a domestic setting were no longer trying to please their men as Katie once did with Oxo gravy; now they used a product like coffee or food or air fresheners or cars to achieve their own ends. It seemed that where once the images had been created for them by commercial expediency, now they were creating their own images to superimpose on the marketplace.

Unlike the feminists, ordinary women who now participated in a real power base had not sought it. It was thrust upon them by the breakdown of the old male-orientated systems which organised society. It was inevitable, though, that women, now politically dominant, needed their own forms of authority and control to maintain some form of government for the country. Popular culture dealt with neither ideas nor fields of operation to help women deal with what they had become. Women had nothing to fall back on except what had empowered them.

Popular culture was the only mass change agent they had experienced. And popular culture can offer only one solution when women seek new directions and frameworks to assert unfamiliar and often alien economic and political power: more of the same. It sets out to make women feel that whatever happens they will be secure.

Cometh the moment, cometh the man. Enter Tony Blair.

By the time Margaret Thatcher left office, image had virtually replaced the concept of party politics. Blair took over this process where she left off. The process of creating government as part of popular culture had a brief gestation period under John Major, who projected almost no image at all. Then, in 1997, as leader of a party reborn from the ashes of old concepts of Labour and Conservative as a kind of political hybrid, Blair became in essence popular culture's first Prime Minister. He described himself as a social democrat; the *Financial Times* described him as a populist, which was probably more prescient than it knew.

It was, incidentally, women who voted for him over-whelmingly – the same ordinary women who had voted first for Mrs Thatcher.

Tony Blair had sought popular-culture credentials from the early days of his career. At school, he is said to have modelled himself on Mick Jagger. Before going up to university, he spent a year in London trying to find fame as a rock promoter. Then, as a student he played guitar and sang with a rock band, and dated future *American Psycho* director Mary Harron. He married Cherie Booth, the daughter of actor Tony Booth. When he first stood as a Labour candidate for Sedgefield, *Coronation Street* actress Pat Phoenix, his father-in-law's girlfriend, helped him in his campaign.

As Prime Minister, Tony Blair was from the start popular culture's creature. He knew immediately that this would be the source of his power. At an inaugural party at Number 10 soon after his election, he invited pop musicians and actors rather than figures from big business or government to launch his prime-ministerial career.

He also had long-standing and close connections with media mogul Rupert Murdoch, who put the weight of his globally influential News Corporation behind Blair, specifically popular-culture purveyor the *Sun*. There is no question that the support of Murdoch's mass-circulation tabloid played an enormous part in Blair's election victories.

As Leader of the Opposition, according to the Commons register of interests, Tony Blair had been Murdoch's guest in Hayman Island. This can be taken to suggest that Blair was always aware of the electoral advantages of being seen to represent the mass electorate as an icon of popular culture rather than as a party politician.

In effect, he turned government into a form of popular culture. To the mass of women voters, he stepped into the role vacated under Margaret Thatcher by men and the male hierarchy. He offered them the impression that they were protected in the face of chaos. He was the personification of the care and protection which popular culture has always given the impression that it offers women.

He actually talked like a messiah, with biblical cadence and rising and falling sentences which often, if you wrote them down, simply trailed into meaninglessness on a rational level. They weren't meaningless, though: like Noel Coward's cheap music, they evoked potent emotion, the emotion of power. Without making any broader comparisons, the fascist dictators of the 1930s and later on the Reverend Ian Paisley were said to sway their audiences with similar quasi-musical transports. In the months following his election in May 1997, Blair recorded the highest approval ratings of any previous British Prime Minister or party leader of either party.

As Prime Minister, surrounded by women Cabinet members whom the media called 'Blair's Babes' and who looked startlingly like an experiment in cloning, Tony Blair as benevolent mentor pushed government into the traditional role of popular culture.

There was nothing ostensibly macho about what he said or did. Just as many women saw Margaret Thatcher as an ersatz male, so Tony Blair seemed strongly in touch with his feminine side. He did not look physically strong. His was a kind of pre-pubertal charm which made women feel that he was 'safe'. He appealed to young, middle-aged and older ordinary women who were looking for a role model on the popular-culture-perfect-family-scene level of *My Family* on TV, or a Cilla Black song. The electorate knew him so well. He popped up on the media like Puck. In what seemed like daily appearances on television, in his interviews in the newspapers – Meet The Real Tony Blair – he sold himself like a product to millions as someone they could relate to instantly, that Nice Mr Blair next door. Of course he had a team of publicity men and press agents, and, yes, make-up artists (he was not above dyeing his hair), honing and selling exactly that message, and it worked. He appeared sincere, caring, nice, friendly, one of us. Above all, he always gave the impression that he was a happy man, with the rider that he could make you happy too. And he always seemed to have time for the ordinary people, in spite of being so busy running the country. He appeared in cameo roles on television – in *The Amazing Mrs Pritchard*, for instance, about an ordinary housewife becoming Prime Minister, which illustrates the point. He was also a 'celebrity' judge on *Masterchef At Large.*

Popular culture became indistinguishable from government. It moved beyond its mind-changing purpose in empowering and then politicising women. It began to dictate to this huge constituency how they should act and behave. Largely without debate in Parliament, Blair began to interfere in areas of people's personal and family lives, with legislation governing how people discipline their children, the food they ate, their health and their safety. He gave the impression that he had to make an effort not to be patronising.

So not only was this form of popular-culture-cum-government promoting and expanding consumer markets, it was now setting out what that market should do and be. Blair manipulated the media to create a distinct community defined in terms of popular culture. It was, indeed, social democracy, but not in an ideological form that a Social Democrat in Germany or Italy or Sweden would recognise as related to professional party politics.

As legislation limited the people's rights to make their own decisions about their families and the way they related to the community, so did the Blair government give them the illusion that they could have their say about what was happening in the country. TV began to broadcast video slots made by members of the public to air their views; a feature of most magazine-style TV programmes, such as BBC's *Breakfast* and ITV's *GMTV*, continually invites e-mail comments from viewers, some of which are read out as a reflection of public opinion. The public was even asked to send in questions for interviewers to ask politicians in the studio, which makes things very easy for the interviewer, who scarcely has to engage in the interview. It made things easy for the politicians, too, who could disarm any attack by promising to look into individual cases of governmental incompetence later on.

Popular culture's celebrities began to take on the role of a sounding board for government policy. Even soap operas set out to find public favour for political policies by using the popularity of much-loved characters – like Charlie Fairhead in *Casualty* – to become part of the political process with scripts showing the complex consequences of government's NHS strategy on funding and cost-cutting. It seemed as if the Blair government was using popular mass-market forms of popular culture as a way of appearing to keep in touch with ordinary people. In *Holby City* and *The Bill*, among others, arguments in the storylines gave the impression that the programmes were a testing ground for whether or not a policy on health or policing would play with the public.

Often, too, there was an impression that Tony Blair and his chief spin doctor, former tabloid journalist Alastair Campbell, were prepared to use popular culture to appeal to the public over the heads of Parliament. In this way, the emotional case could be won before reason entered the debate. In 2003, the *Daily Telegraph* quoted John Major: 'Blair's spin is the porn of politics.'

But the crucial moment when the dividing line between

traditional government and popular culture was finally obliterated came early in Tony Blair's premiership, with the death of Princess Diana. In an emotional speech on the morning of her death in August 1997, he spoke of her as 'The People's Princess', and in so doing claimed her as popular culture's first public martyr. The TV audience for her wedding had been 750 million worldwide; 2.5 billion watched her funeral.

Diana was a powerful popular-culture icon; she was also its creature. She was much loved, but evidently the public – particularly women – never examined the real person behind who or what it was they so loved and admired.

She ticked all the popular-culture boxes, of course. She was attractive, but not in any extraordinary way. Ordinary women could aspire to look like her, and, indeed, many of them did. She was also the proof, if proof were needed, that fashion and beauty and health fads and pop music and publicity and shopping, too, were powerful agents in creating a successful public persona; these filled her life as it was presented to us to support the mythic 'People's Princess'. In the public eye, fed by women's obsession with Diana's perfect popular-culture image and her undoubted skill at manipulating that image, she was a Cinderella, transformed from a shy helper in a nursery school into the most quintessential celebrity in the world.

In a way, in ignoring the reality – the titled family, Althorp House, the wealth, the habit of privilege – behind this image, the public en masse chose to put the popular culture image above real life. In accepting the image as the 'truth', reality was defeated. It did not seem to occur to anyone that the real woman was swallowed up by the image. In fact Diana herself fed the public greed for that image.

Millions of women identified with her as a mother defending her sons against the forces of the Establishment; they related to her as a wronged woman. Women universally seemed to forgive her everything, including her taste for other women's husbands, her obscene extravagance, her self-pity. She was a victim of the system; she suffered on a large-scale public screen as millions of other women suffered unseen in their ordinary lives, but those women could not speak out and become popular culture's metaphor for women's pain. Diana, the popular-culture martyr, was a powerful metaphor for victimised womanhood.

When she died – 'murdered by the media' with Dodi Al Fayed, a scion of that commercial Palace of Culture, Harrods – women turned to the mass media to demand reassurance that she had been destroyed by forces outside their own security zone – they demanded illusions. Hence the media conspiracy theories, blaming various plots emanating from the Establishment and the security services. This kind of speculative sensationalism, the intensity of prejudice, was the very stuff of popular culture, it provided the media's obvious explanation. And if she wasn't killed by those who feared the enormous emotive power of her media image, who did kill her? There was little emotional mileage to be made from a tragic, stupid traffic accident involving a drunk driver. It was unthinkable that popular culture – and by association the mass of the public them-selves – could be implicated as an agent of her martyrdom.

Nothing rational could stand in the way of the huge tidal wave of hysterical emotion which swept the country after her death. And Tony Blair conducted the public response like an orchestra. Even that genuine public grief was part of a broader political contrivance, milked and manipulated for commercial ends. Popular culture used the Diana of its own creation, and particularly her death, as a very powerful statement about who or what now ran a country dependent on a constituency of politically empowered ordinary women. It wasn't Parliament; it wasn't the Royal Family; it wasn't the civil service or the unions: it was popular culture in all its forms; and its spin doctors, the commercial tough guys who profited from it.

As a result, government became openly reactive. Now all major parliamentary decisions are designed to meet public approval, which is not the same thing at all as the public good. Again and again legislation which would reduce human rights, for example, is introduced on the basis that this is what the public wants, with no other evidence of need or advantage. One example of this was the debacle over extending the period of questioning of terrorists to forty-two days. In several cases, as in this, the approval-seeking government has been thwarted in its populist policies by the more rational House of Lords, which appears to be the one area of Parliament where popular culture's influence has not yet gained sway.

This mass-popularity factor can be seen in action in the way government ministers appear on BBC's *Breakfast* or ITV's *GMTV* to 'explain' policy plans which will be announced officially later that day. On the television, the early policy announcement is taken to constitute the 'news value' of the item; there is rarely any real attempt on the part of reporters to question the content. How can they, it hasn't been released for them to read? By the time it is, it is old news. So government goes unchallenged and a *fait accompli* is created.

You can call this the viable dissemination of information,

I suppose, and dismiss it as no cause for serious concern. At the most trivial level, the public accepts without question when some law to change an aspect of anti-social behaviour is brought in – using a mobile phone when driving, for instance – which is impossible to police adequately and to apply. Patently, the evidence of our own eyes tells us that it is not possible. But we seem to feel protected simply by the existence of even bad law.

The essential problem with government by popular culture is that no one is made to take responsibility for the consequences of political policy. If all governmental policy is seen to be approved by the mass of people, and all government, of whatever colour, is made up of politicians who operate on the emotional, anti-cerebral level of those people, not only is there very little electoral choice between political party ideology, there is also less chance that government can ever break out of the downward spiral as popular culture seeks ever more approval-seeking levels.

There is no sign that this downward spiral will be broken soon. There is no indication of any large-scale public interest in questioning where society is heading. We still give image priority over reality. We have come a long way since John Kennedy was virtually voted President of the United States because he 'looked more attractive' on television than Richard Nixon. Nixon, literally, did not put on make-up; Kennedy did, and so he struck a chord of recognition with the electorate; he appeared in their sitting rooms looking like a soap star. Nixon, sweating and unshaven, looked like the villain in a crime series who had spent the night in a police cell.

The alliance between popular culture and government has become both more sophisticated and more simplistic.

Today it goes without saying that politicians' battles for electoral support are fought and won by the skill of spin doctors appealing direct by screen or written word to the emotions of the electorate. People in power know already that for the mass of people they reach, the issue is not what they say, but the way that they say it; political power becomes a process of seduction, not persuasion.

11

Once government joined forces with popular culture as a political instrument to control society, politicians began to 'communicate' practical authority as though they were directing a TV soap opera.

One inevitable effect of this is that the information we are given is selective; another is that policy is geared to a mass section of the electorate who have been 'groomed' by the united resources of popular culture to accept it. The government sees its function as simply to be approved. As a result, government concentrates its activities on what concerns only part, albeit a majority, of the population. That majority also represents those who have gained the power to influence political policy by a means that ensures they have the least possible capacity to criticise and challenge what the government does.

In the last decade we have seen how this reduces a government's responsibility to the electorate as a whole. For example, this is evident in the way over ten years the current government has marginalised agriculture and rural affairs in favour of urban issues. Popular culture's constituency is overwhelmingly urban or suburban, and, of course, it is largely made up of the women empowered by it. So the media covers rural life in terms of issues like the environment and cheap food which are the sole considerations to people who do not live and work anywhere near agricultural areas; and when it comes to pure farming, central government is primarily influenced by the interests of the supermarkets.

This is not a question of whether politicians are right or wrong in their priorities. It is simply an example of how government performs reactively, and quite possibly against the interests of an important industry, in this case agriculture, so as to manipulate the perceptions of the electorate.

Panic decisions often seem to be made solely on the basis of keeping the consumer happy. In consequence, political decision-making and debate are automatically dumbed-down to the acceptance levels of the lowest common denominator, which is the inclusive level which makes sure that the greatest number of voters are included. In this case, this applies to those most profoundly shaped by popular culture's effects, and therefore least likely to engage logic or intellectual debate in their judgements. This is compounded because these are probably policy issues about which the majority of the public knows little or nothing in factual terms. And, as we have seen, their access to such factual or expert information becomes increasingly difficult because the mass media controls knowledge which might make government appear in a bad light.

In practice, like the daytime-TV executives who set out in the Sixties to attract untapped audiences of women in their own homes, the politicians now target the ordinary women who can be reached through their emotions. These emotions, incidentally, include fear. This is useful to government as a facet of controlling the public mood to its own ends – as was shown during the Home Office campaign for forty-two days' detention for terror suspects, which was based on unashamed overstating of a terrorist threat.

Nor have the methods politicians use essentially changed

from the early television chiefs; they, too, use melodrama and exaggeration to bypass logic and to play on public emotion by increasing fear and emphasising risk. In doing so, popular-culture-style images are used to manipulate the public into believing that what the government has to offer is what they want. For example, there are several cases of teenagers being stabbed to death; the government brings out a public service advertising campaign warning kids against carrying knives; the public – not the kids – see this as government action: Government takes on the role of the people's support system.

So the electorate are encouraged to see themselves as victims; they become the poor and deprived, the put-upon women whose husbands beat them or abandon the family . . . In a weird way this works to unite the public as a kind of community; the vast majority who are not real-life victims sympathise with the suffering fellow citizens they see and hear and read about in the media, and feel protective towards those apparently more vulnerable than themselves. The electorate accepts a form of institutionalisation. This is very close to brainwashing.

A case in point is the question of making funding available to women with children. Here popular mis-conception can distort reality. Dr Catherine Hakim, Senior Research Fellow at the London School of Economics, has argued that money is poured into daycare simply because many mothers work. This sidesteps the question of whether women would rather have the money to be at home with their children. Dr Hakim's research shows that in Britain 20 per cent of women give priority to careers; 20 per cent give priority to children and family and do not work outside the home; 60 per cent combine work and family life. She claims that too often policies for mothers are based on the work-centred 20 per cent on whom the media concentrates, regardless of either of the other groups' actual preferences.

It's easy enough to sound alarm bells about populist government, but such fears will have little effect on the women who have been politically empowered by pop culture to see themselves in a special relationship with a government which appears to want them to be happy. Why should they question whether this is dangerous? They believe the mass media without question because what the media tells them is what they want to hear.

In reality, though, we can now begin to see the limitations of political power based on popular culture when applied to playing a controlling role in the government of the country.

Popular culture is by definition aimed to please. It has no means to make demands on ordinary women to think outside the box; or to enable them to break away from the emotional bonding process by which it exercises its power.

12

Who and what, then, are the women who now hold crucial political power? And what are they going to do with it?

The answer to that is, sadly, that they have no idea. Many feminists who recognised that their dreams of government of the female by the female for the female would never be realised simply by destroying the male bases of society, must be horribly disappointed by how little society has changed by being feminised by ordinary women. The huge constituency of these women have made life easier for themselves, perhaps, but the 1970s issues of family, childcare, equal pay, flexible working hours, sexual harassment at work, are still major preoccupations for politicians and unions and business. Appointments like that of Sara Payne – who's eight-year-old daughter was tragically murdered by a paedophile – as Minister for Victims is typical, a patch of emotional carpet on the same worn old treadmill. Do even women want official sanction for a Ministry of Victims?

If the system is essentially unchanged, though, ordinary women do not see themselves as unchangeable.

For half a century they have automatically accepted as their own the images and definitions of themselves they see reflected through popular culture. There would seem to be an evolutionary difference between the attitudes of women in the Sixties and now. They look different, they sound different, they do things differently. Even so, we have to question whether the apparent change in self-image wrought by popular culture for the mass of women is real, or simply an illusion given credence because, for commercial expediency, it is perceived to be real by the mass of the population. The entire process of change which popular culture made possible for women is based on renewing their image, both in reality and in their wishful thinking. They create a definition of change by simply looking in the mirror.

In the early days, the first generation we talked about saw different women's lives reflected through the media, and could thereby imagine other ways they could aspire to live. In the second generation, we saw younger women using popular culture to create images for themselves. Or, at least, to create themselves *as* popular-culture images. That gave them the illusion that the image was real – 'I look like a celebrity, therefore I am.'

Popular culture uses and creates images, but these are all applied; it does not involve the creative imaginations of its consumers; it provides guidelines of its own for them, rather as children colour in pre-drawn outlines when they start to paint.

These women have always been sold the image which would maximise commercial markets for popular culture's 'products'. This has given them real economic importance, but it has not provided any means for them to use their power in any creative way. Nor, in the drive to make them spend, has it provided them with any sense of responsibility or self-reliance about what they do.

Popular culture's aspirational image for women is subjective, and it is internalised. It creates a stereotypical popular-culture persona, and vast numbers of young women tap into that. Those who have not, or who cannot conform to that criterion, are effectively outsiders whose resistance to the stereotype is swamped by the weight of numbers of the in-crowd.

As women grow older popular culture loses interest in them. They may maintain their spending levels as consumers, but they are not fresh meat for the media market, with its enthusiasm for the new. Popular culture is of necessity focused on youth.

We have seen that the second generation of women empowered by popular culture – the baby-boomers – were different from the first. Tom Wolfe called those who were in their popular-culture prime from the late 1960s to the mid-Eighties the Me Generation. Popular concerns shifted then from a woman's social development beyond the family to a mass selfish focus on individual well-being. Popular culture encouraged the young women involved to define themselves in terms of self-absorption. Global and even national concepts were too vague and too cerebral to connect with these young women. They were looking for sensual sensation, for self-exploration and self-experiment; a kind of epiphany of self.

These women lived for now, and in the now they had no sense of social responsibility, nor desire to make comparisons between themselves and anyone older. As for a sense of community, it was more important to concentrate on knowing oneself. How can you love anyone else if you don't love yourself? Self-criticism makes you dysfunctional, so there is no criticism.

For these women the future did not exist, only the present, and the present was filled by self-expression within the context of fashion, photography, advertising and sex. Young women talked a lot about love; they explored all aspects of sex searching for it, wrote the word on their foreheads, wore it on their T-shirts; but it was just another pathway to love of self. Children, community, social responsibility? As American Secretary for Defence Donald Rumsfeld said about the aftermath of the invasion of Iraq, 'stuff happens'. This second generation, the Me Generation, are now the mothers of another generation, the young women of today called by the media 'Millennials'. These are perhaps the real victims of the way popular culture empowered their mothers.

Popular culture provided ordinary women of the Me Generation with no blueprint for giving love. Receiving it, as an entitlement to love of self, yes, but love of a child which perforce sets up a barrier to self-centredness? A child is responsibility; maternity demands a relationship with a community. The ordinary women of the Me Generation had not been nurtured to face this, even if the majority did vaguely expect to marry and start families one day. That day was always later, when their own lives, as they saw it, would be over.

So one is forced to the conclusion that many of today's young female Millennials were not much loved in the old-fashioned sense of being put first by self-absorbed mothers in a real-life mother-daughter family relationship. Not in the way those second-generation mothers had been loved by their own mothers, who had still expected to give priority to their children over their own interests. Their reward was that those daughters tended to experience that love as controlling, and their rebellion against parental caring was to cut loose to be themselves.

This does not necessarily mean that the Millennials' mothers did not go through the motions of love. They had simply cut themselves off from the ability to offer the experience of mature inter-generational love. Many used their children as an extension of their quest for self-love and looked to compensate through them for their own disappointed expectations. Looking back, they saw their own failure as caused by lack of confidence in themselves, or want of opportunity, so they made up for that in bolstering the self-esteem of the new generation. In that scenario, criticism has no place. There is no constructive criticism; anything but admiring praise is an attack on that carefully nurtured self-esteem.

From this, no doubt, stemmed all those pushy mothers, the mothers from hell, who created the pathetic Stepford children of child beauty contests. Nor did this form of popular-culture-driven mothering make the children loving. They did not respect their mothers' way of loving them, and they had no experience of real emotional commitment to pass on to their own children when they had them. The women of the Me Generation, as they got older, may even have subscribed to the advertising images of happy motherhood; to promises of fulfilling relationships in the mass-market magazines; but there was no substance to the image, the media was still the message. It bore no relation to reality. These women's own knowledge revolved around self. Reality was something entirely different, but reality was what real parenting required.

Take three actual cases: the first from a single mother, a successful novelist, whose thirteen-year-old daughter regularly brought older teenagers home to sleep with her. 'I tried to stop her, but she just stayed out and I didn't know where she was. At least if I make them welcome I know where she is. No, she's not on the Pill; I'd never pollute her young body with chemicals . . . '.

The second is an older-than-average mother who dedicated

herself for nearly a year to doing her daughter's practical course work for GCE 'A' Level so that the girl would get the grades required to get into university. 'I want her to go there to live every moment and have a wonderful time. I don't want her to spend her time studying to get any sort of qualification for a career. All that can come later if she wants. This is a time she should enjoy herself and be proud to be herself.'

The third is a single mother, a nurse, who split with her partner of several years because he questioned the way she brought up her schoolgirl daughters from a previous relationship. She said, 'He thinks I give them too much freedom, and that I do too much for them. I want them to do everything they want while they're young so they enjoy themselves while they can, before they have to think about growing up. So they hated Ian because he told them what to do, when he wasn't even their father. He thought I should lay down rules to stop them having all their friends in when I'm out working because they bring in booze and trash the place. The neighbours complain and call the police but I can't stop them bringing their friends in, can I? I want them to enjoy themselves while they can.'

The children of these women, the generation who are young women now, are paying a price for such indulgence. Without traditional connection with their mothers, and with no practice in relationships outside their peer group, now they in their turn are looking to popular culture to fulfil the human need to feel loved.

They are, as an age group, hard to provide with love. They not only take any effort to relate to them as part of their entitlement, but they have nothing meaningful to offer in return. Brought up on what is called in media studies research 'tot-level self-esteem boosterism', this generation of young women feels free to behave as if they ruled the world, except they have no idea what the world involves. Every aspect of popular culture reinforces their sense of their own importance, because they are the new market; and new technology has ensured that they represent a growth potential which makes them economically vital to society as a whole. To an extent, we have to take them at their own inflated self-valuation because to question it, and deflate their self-belief, threatens the future of all of us. We are dependent on their arrogance and sense of entitlement as a new growth market for popular culture for economic stability. For the foreseeable future (two years at least) they are where the money is.

This is beyond dispute, and en masse they not only know it, they take it for granted. They feel they are owed. As far as this group is concerned, there is no world beyond themselves. To quote an article in the *Christian Science Monitor*, 'Why are younger Americans so miserable?' the Millennials are characterised by 'luxury-as-necessity entitlement', and what media academics apparently call 'instant fame-ification', which seems to mean the right to be plucked from nowhere to popular-culture celebrity as a supermodel or a pop idol or a soap star. A 2007 report from the United States, entitled *Egos Inflating Over Time*, points to this new generation's lack of empathy, and an inability to form relationships. What emerges from any scrutiny of young people today is 'an inappropriate application of self-esteem'. The research study claimed that 30 per cent more college students showed 'elevated narcissism' in 2006 compared with 1982.

This research involved American college students, but

there's no reason to think Britain's young people are any different. Technology has created popular culture as something truly global. If anything, the welfare state in Britain has probably reinforced the expectations raised by popular culture to create an even stronger self-belief and sense of entitlement than in the USA where, at the end of the day, the state does not provide. In America the need to survive will compel the narcissists there at least to go through the motions of some sense of personal responsibility; but not here. In Britain, if you believe that the world owes you a living, the world will ultimately cough up.

According to Jean Twenge, a psychology professor at San Diego University, and lead author of the American report, these 'Millennials' are 'full-blown narcissists'.

Professor Twenge told the *Monitor*, 'Research shows narcissists are aggressive when they have been insulted or threatened. They tend to have problems with impulse control . . .'

And you only have to watch *The X-Factor* or *Big Brother* to see evidence of narcissistic contestants' aggression when they feel insulted or their self-esteem is threatened by rejection.

The wider social implications of this will be dealt with later, but for now it is as well to try to understand the phenomenon in human, personal terms through a single case.

A sociologist friend wrote to me recently to tell me about Jessica, her first lodger. This is a typical Millennial.

'Jessica is an Essex girl. She looked fine. Tall, a bit hefty, good-looking. In fact, rather pretty. She was twenty-seven. She said she worked in public relations. She seemed happy, confident, pleasantly simple. But then I'd never met a ladette before. I didn't even know what one was. Then she moved in, took off her jacket to reveal what she called "these puppies" bursting from her inadequate brassiere, had her hair dyed blonde, and unleashed the contents of Primark so that when she "got ready", which is what these girls do, she looked like an immense toddler. She'd pop into the sitting-room before she went out to show herself to me.

'She had lots of friends. The girls were all small, weaselly looking creatures, the men ditto, and uniformly homosexual. She called them all "Monkey". Anyway Jessica filled her room with Primark garments all over the floor and gushing out of drawers (she was pathologically incapable of closing doors and drawers) and cuddly toys. Oh, and a large print of Marilyn Monroe, with whom she claimed affinity, on the wall. One evening one of the weasels brought in another weasel. This new aspirant gazed admiringly at Jessica and asked if she met anyone nice off the Internet. Not really, said Jessica, but you get an awful lot of fucks.

'Her public relations work turned out to be cold-calling, selling insurance. She was the boss, in charge of thirty or so other cold-callers, many of whom she was particularly proud to say were men older than herself. She was on £45,000 a year, and owed £25,000. She knew she had overspent, but she didn't seem to know how. She did, however, know her job. Her speciality was keeping her staff up to the mark. Whenever she sensed slacking was on the cards, she'd announce there'd be a chocolate bar for the one who sold most insurance at the end of the day. All she had to do was nip to the sweet shop, buy the chocolate bar and put it on her desk. She said it made the hell of a difference. Every month or so they held an employee of the month gala evening. Jessica came home from her personal victory celebration with a Woolworth tiara which

139

she placed among her other souvenirs and wore to many other festivities.

'Jessica always picked up the tab when she went out clubbing. She told me this quite impatiently, as though she wondered who the hell I thought might pick up the tab. Hence the many weasels, I suppose. She got up on tables and danced, waved her arms in the air and bounced her puppies. She had a high degree of self-esteem. Hers lay in her sense of self-definition. She was a "Buddhist" and a "vegetarian". She had a Buddha figurine to which she chanted piercingly for three-quarters of an hour at a time. I asked her to tell me the meaning of the chant. Oh, she said, it just means gimme what I want. She said if you keep it up for long enough it's better than coke. Her eating habits were gross. Family size pizzas for the most part, with a smear of tomato sauce and mozzarella, she'd have to cut the edges off to get in the oven. Everything she ate was pre-cooked and full of E-numbers. Once she saw me cutting up a chicken. She gagged and flounced out of the kitchen. Once I said something about couldn't she get a bit more on her plate if she tried. Four days later she came into the sitting room looking grim. Nobody, she said, talks to her like that. Nobody. Her friends had been shocked. I must have looked a bit lost. "You know I have eating issues," she explained. And began again, with emphases. "Nobody talks to ME like that. NOBODY talks to ME like that. My friends were SHOCKED."

'I was quite fond of Jessica. She had moved here because of a bust-up with a boyfriend who had become dangerously violent. She said she hated her mother "because she's a cow", and loved her father who was married to a girl her age.

'I didn't know about the computer dating for months on

account of her using the basement entrance straight into her boudoir. She was perfectly straight about it when I asked. She never saw them more than once, she said, as though this ameliorated the habit. Yes, this morning she walked her beau to the taxi office round the corner and he held out his hand and said "nice meeting you". Still, he was a good fuck. I don't know when I heard such pathos as the "nice meeting you" farewell. Or a more self-deluding bit of bravado.

'She agreed with me when I suggested she'd be happier in a self-contained flat. After she'd gone I had to pay a refuse collector to take away the trash she left behind. Including the brand new IKEA day bed, now with its iron frame curlicues literally snapped asunder. It was a bit embarrassing when he moved the bloody thing as underneath lay a heap of used condoms. I felt ashamed of my gender. I never heard from her.'

If nothing else, this illustrates the gulf of understanding between the Millennials and the older generation. Where once the simple fact of being female would have provided a basis for understanding, now the expansion of the popular culture women shared, even if they related to it differently, is driving them apart. My friend had expected to be able to relate to a young woman like Jessica because she remembers what it felt like to be young herself. She looked for common ground, expecting a common basic sense of female morality in a social context. The girl's amorality scared her. Not personally, but because of the future impact of an amoral generation on society.

It's hard not to anticipate the tragedy awaiting this new young generation when – or if – reality kicks in. No one can fail to be depressed by the abyss that exists in real life between what they have been nurtured to believe they can have, and what they are actually equipped to have any chance of achieving.

That is scary enough, but worse still – indeed almost sinister – is the way popular culture, allied with new technology, has created a device whereby millions of Millennials may be able to avoid ever having to confront reality at all.

The mass media, having empowered women and created a generation of narcissists who cannot relate to other people; who identify themselves in terms of what they feel and look like; who have been brought up not to think but to feel, has now followed the market (and the dream) into a kind of parallel world which coexists within the wider society, but makes it possible to avoid having to relate to it in real, direct, terms. It has reinvented these young people's world for them in its own image.

This parallel life is lived via the Internet and the world wide web. Facebook and My Space and Twitter, personal blogs and message boards, and role-playing web sites like Second Life make it possible for popular culture's long-standing promises to come true. Ordinary people can Live the Dream in a virtual world. These Internet sites, called MUDs – Multi-User Dungeons – allow users to create their own characters to interact with other users, and play out their fantasies as an alter ego. Many women apparently say that they have felt liberated when signing on as a man.

This Internet facility has gone much further than simply using social networking sites to create a fictional persona and communicate without the constraints and limitations of truth. At least the fictional persona holds an element of reality – the real person released to be themselves.

Perhaps no one could have anticipated the extent to which

Millennials embraced the opportunity to express themselves to, and demand the attention of, a worldwide audience of billions through personal blogs and Facebook, MySpace and the rest. Commercial businesses and social psychologists have praised role-playing games like Second Life for connecting people, but the British charity Relate has said that its counsellors were coming across an increasing number of people whose real-life relationships were falling apart because of what was happening in their parallel, unreal, worlds.

The Second Life virtual world enables players to create an alter-ego, or avatar, which can move around the virtual world socialising, setting up businesses with virtual currency, the Linden $, and falling in love. In Second Life Amy Taylor, 28, from Cornwall, is a club DJ called Laura Skye. She met her unemployed husband, David Pollard, 40, in an Internet chatroom, and as Laura Skye teamed up with his Second Life alter-ego, Dave Barmy, who lives in a winter chalet with a Cobra helicopter gunship parked outside. In real life they married in 2005, and lived in Newquay.

Then Amy Taylor caught her husband at the computer watching Dave Barmy having Second Life sex with a prostitute. Amy ended her on-line relationship with Dave, but stayed with Pollard. But then she turned to a virtual female private eye who set up a honey-trap for Barmy. He passed that test, talking about Laura Skye all night, but later Amy found Barmy chatting in cyber-space to another woman. She suspected that Pollard was having a real relationship with the human controlling the other woman. In real life, Amy filed for divorce.

Even Amy Taylor called the saga 'bizarre'. 'People find love in lots of different ways,' she said.

Second Life was set up in 2003, and in 2008 had fifteen

million registered accounts, with thirty-eight thousand 'residents' logged in at any one moment. There are several similar Internet sites available.

This is a new departure for popular culture, perhaps, but it was always a logical emotional leap from *Coronation Street* creator Bill Podmore's initial criterion for appealing to the hearts and minds of ordinary women: 'satisfied wives and mothers are boring . . . '

Mitch Kapor, former chairman of the firm who created Second Life, Linden Labs, was well aware of how popular culture had operated on millions of ordinary people so that they were ready to inhabit a virtual world. Speaking at the celebration of the company's fifth birthday party, he said: 'In the earliest wave of pioneers in any new disruptive platform, the marginal and dispossessed are over-represented; not the sole constituents by any means, but people who feel they don't fit, who have nothing left to lose, or who were impelled by some kind of dream, who may be outsiders to whatever mainstream they are coming from, all come and arrive early in disproportionate numbers.'

One element of the role which the Internet has taken on is to replace actual relationships between real women, and between generations. The Internet performs the 'friendship function'. This may lead to a greater level of candour and criticism when comment can be handed out anonymously and without comeback on blogs and chat lines rather than face to face with a real person who might react with anger or distress. And then the world wide web lacks central administration, and operates outside many legal controls. Things can be said and freely talked about that could not be said amongst a group of actual people. With the new web access via personal devices like mobile phones and datacards, it is uniquely personal and unsupervised. This can be divisive for women, who find aggression and criticism difficult to take even within a relationship where they know they are loved and cared about. The random, often intimate, reactions of people on the Internet can be unsettling. And divisive, too, fostering as it does suspicion and even fear among older women because they cannot easily communicate with what can seem like people without familiar human characteristics.

Via the Internet, technology has developed media formats which have cultivated a new generation of young women who, in real terms, operate openly as figments of their own popular-culture dreams.

The mass media and their peer groups may love these Millennials, but beyond that they have lost most of women's traditional connections with older members of their own sex. Older women, in this context, may still be in their thirties.

The mass media, with its promotion of image identification, loses interest in older generations as each new group with fresh commercial potential comes along. Popular culture is constantly reminding women, once they are in their thirties, that they are no longer interesting or a stimulus to innovation. The media does not want to remind its new target market that the party will soon be over. For a while, advertisers and the retail industry can still make money out of this older market by selling products making unreal promises that they can look young again and rejoin Life with a capital L, but this is a side issue. Older women can even go on Second Life and live a virtual life as a sixteen-year-old celebrity. But for those who have already lived through their own popular-culture generation, the dream is always harder to believe. Older women have what the Millennials do not, yet – real lives as well as dreams. But as far as popular culture is concerned, they do not count.

This lack of mass-media significance is not only because the consumer profile of women outside the target market becomes less profitable, though this is important. Older women also become more sceptical, forced by the circumstances of maturity to face reality. They have family and social functions with which they find that the aspirational promises of popular culture have not prepared them to cope. The scriptwriters of *Popular Culture*, the Soap Opera, have lost interest in their storyline and moved on. And since popular culture has now been in the position of setting definitions for these older women for decades, they feel like TV soap stars who have been written out and are now looking for work, any work at all. Their isolation is made worse because as people they have few resources outside popular culture to fall back on.

Popular culture has also flourished by fuelling an innate hostility between women. This may stem from a primitive instinct to protect children who might be supplanted by the offspring of a younger rival, but it has persisted over the centuries in women's relationships with each other in the family and at work. Popular culture has always known how to manipulate it, fostering envy at all levels of feminine display as a market stimulus. So the mass media mocked the feminists; it reduced old women en masse to purposeless images of senility or infantile helplessness; it defined mature wives and mothers as kill-joys or self-flagellists repelled by their own image in the mirror.

That is to say, in popular culture none of these groups are positive role models as soon as they no longer fit the mass-market target in-crowd, and they are unrewarding in media terms. The young want to forget that they exist. To them, middle-aged emotion is embarrassing; middle-aged sexuality seems gross and their pleasures unexciting. So mature women are perceived as lacking all the potential for sensual melodrama and extreme emotion by which mass media survives and grows.

This hostility between women exists but older women will often deny that it does. Older women have never been more wary of the younger generation than they are in the first decade of the twenty-first century. They resent younger women's selfishness, their sense of entitlement, their lack of interest in anything outside their own existence. They forget, of course, that they themselves were similarly disliked by generations previous to themselves.

Frankly, they are jealous.

Jealousy is not the same as envy. Creating envy between women was, and is, fundamental to popular culture's methodology, a way of boosting aspirational spending.

Jealousy, though, is something else. It is wholly self-destructive, an obsessional fear of losing what older women once believed was theirs. Such women are facing the loss of what popular culture gave them, their self image, even their identity. The popular culture which empowered them offers no solution to this loss. It has no means to protect them because in its terms they have become boring, their experience limited to what is already old-fashioned and uninteresting.

Of course they are boring only in popular-culture perception; in real life they may be on the brink of becoming interesting as they start to face reality.

Even so, it is popular culture which is calling the tune.

13

This then is the political constituency of the ordinary women who have been empowered over half a century; a female society defined by different generations' experiences of popular culture. And, because it is the nature of popular culture that it continuously grows out of the ashes of its own previous existence, these women form a powerful grouping within which each generation communicates laterally with its peers, but where there is little understanding or connection with those older or younger than themselves.

This is not to suggest that the way the mass of women have been manipulated is due to lack of intelligence on their part but popular culture by its nature goes out of its way *not* to activate the intelligence of its consumers, because once rational questioning or judgement is involved, the sentimental soufflé of its content collapses.

One cannot even argue that women have been remiss that they have let themselves be used, for that's not the case either. As ordinary women, they could do nothing else. Their source of information and of experience was dictated by popular culture. Empowered and politicised by the mass media, they can only respond to what is done in their name in the context of facts as popular culture provides them. That is all they have to go on.

Popular culture has presided over a kind of mass suspension of disbelief in our society. This effect depends on overwhelming its consumers with information which challenges their feelings. The few facts it provides are heavily surcharged with emotional stimuli – as in selective pictures accompanying news in the newspapers and on television. This is why radio news is much more informative than other media.

Once the media starts to engage consumers' reason to question that combination of information with imposed emotion – in 'serious' journalism like *The Times Literary Supplement* or the *Financial Times* or Channel Four's *Dispatches*, perhaps – popular culture loses its power to manipulate how they act. But almost inevitably the *mass* media does not engage consumers' reason, only emotion.

This particularly affects women because the mass media is largely targeted at women; and because women make up the majority of its consumers. Also, women have always been more immediately guided by their emotions and feelings than are men. So it is the women whom popular culture has empowered who have been conditioned not to think; not for themselves, anyway. Popular culture provides instead a process of politically correct approval ratings which give an illusion of moral standards for simple judgements of good or bad. It's curious, incidentally, that popular culture, and its main standard-setting devices, political correctness and parental control, all have the same initials – PC – in media shorthand, as though they were synonymous.

Popular culture's moral guidelines – or the appropriate emotional responses – are communicated by the media with uncompromising images of what is or is not acceptable. Judgement is based on degrees of pity or distress generated by pictures of suffering babies; on indignation – stories of uncaring treatment of terminal illness, for example, or self-interest on the part of big business, particularly banks, oil or drug companies; and on fear – over the terrorist threat, for instance, or a growth in feral behaviour among disaffected teenagers.

All this is part of a concerted process of social control. Popular culture manipulates public response to be compliant with what is done (or not done) by government. Local authorities may be the object of emotional dislike within the mass media; but scarcely ever the government.

This may seem odd and highly inappropriate until you remember how closely the process of government and popular culture are associated. Television and newspaper news coverage provides daily illustrations that on a political level they are prepared to protect the government. This shows itself in inept and superficial questioning of officials based on lack of preparation; in allowing government spokesmen to dictate subject matter; and in time limits which prevent any development of questioning.

There is a chance that there is nothing sinister in this and that the media men and women are not particularly good at their jobs. But this cannot be true of all of them, though this would seem to be the case if it is not deliberate media policy to protect the government.

Nevertheless, the days are long gone in journalism when the role of the news media was first and foremost to challenge and check on government and other institutional forms of authority. By this criterion what is happening is simple and cynical dereliction of journalistic duty.

This has been facilitated by a growing perception that the people who carry out the functions of journalism – reporting, presenting, interviewing and so on – are 'celebrities' in their own right, and therefore part of the popular-culture process. Considering the sums of money some of these 'stars' get paid, it is not surprising that they seem happy to embrace the system. Indeed, this must be seen as part of the job. They do not control content; they can only follow the orders of some behind-the-scenes executives who think they are giving the public what it wants.

Now journalism seems to see itself as the government's translation facility. Too many mass-market newspapers are owned by individuals with 'vested interests' in influencing government policy – Rupert Murdoch and the introduction of Sky Television spring to mind. But also an important factor is what is perceived as a need, as political apologists always phrase it, to 'protect the people of this country' from unedited truth. One example of this 'We're in safe hands' media approach is illustrated in a 2007 *Good Housekeeping* interview with Jacqui Smith, then the newly appointed first female Home Secretary.

'She's an *X-Factor* fan, mother of two young boys, a former teacher who supports Aston Villa . . . ' (That's the popular-culture credential established, then.) In the interview itself, Jacqui, looking refreshed and alert after a holiday with the family in their static caravan in Wales, comments on the 'outcry' over her décolletage at the despatch box when she made her first speech as Home Secretary. The camera fixed to the ceiling of the House of Commons gave 'an unfortunately clear view' of the Home Secretary's cleavage as she addressed the House about the latest terror attacks on the UK – and the pictures were what filled the newspapers the following day. 'You've just got to laugh it off,' she says. 'I mean, I'm doing a statement about terrorism and, funnily enough, what was top of my mind when I got up that morning was "What do I need to do to protect the

British people against the terrorist threat?" not "Is this top a bit low cut?" Actually I think people would prefer I concentrate on keeping the UK safe from terrorism rather than what top I should wear. Mind you, I haven't worn it since!'

It's probably unfair to single out this one inane example, but it is a typical illustration of the media's projected comfort factor. It makes the Home Secretary seem like a person as simplistic and ordinary as most of the rest of us. Our feelings are engaged rather than our brains and the feeling generated in the reader is that such a 'nice person' as the Home Secretary won't let us down.

The way popular culture shares information through displays of emotion rather than rational argument raises questions about how it has actually changed our perceptions of truth, and our judgement of right and wrong in the real world.

Consider the way news is increasingly presented, on TV, in the newspapers, or over the Internet. The priority is no longer to inform or provide fact. The media are looking for an image, on the basis that, whatever the facts, image does not lie. But it does not always tell the truth.

In Northern Ireland in the Seventies, where I was a reporter for the *Daily Mirror*, a women's community protest meeting one Sunday in the suburbs of Belfast triggered a riot. The young reporter from one Sunday newspaper, certain that the story would be forgotten by the time he had to file for the next weekend, ignored it. But there was a lot of banging of dustbin lids and children throwing petrol bombs, and the British Army got involved. The daily newspapers, short of copy that day, made a big thing out of it on Monday morning. So, later in the week the Sunday paper reporter took a photographer and persuaded the women to re-enact what had happened for the camera. I don't know if money changed hands, but the women acted with a will. The Army descended. The presence of the camera inspired the 'rioters' to put on more of a show. People were hurt. The Sunday reporter was, of course, the only journalist there. He had an exclusive and kick-started a brilliant career. No one complained because no one questioned the story when it was published with pictures in the newspaper. The contrived image had indeed become the fact.

In principle, the greater the emotion generated, the stronger the moral truth. John Birt, now Lord Birt, consistently argued, when he was Director-General of the BBC, that the right way to present factual news was through 'real' people and their personal stories, rather than through statements or concepts. In effect, this means that coverage of events like floods or large-scale house repossession or a train crash becomes a small human facet of a large event. It was a very long time indeed, for instance, before the so-called news channels or the tabloid newspapers covering flood disasters in the Tewkesbury area and in Hull in 2007 began to ask challenging questions about government policy allowing the building of housing estates on flood plains. Our attention had been concentrated wholly on a few individual families' horrible struggle against the sludge, or others' problem with insurance.

This is exactly popular culture's way with broad issues, and, though an individual's tragedy makes a good, emotion-filled, human story, it reveals only a fraction of the truth about a serious issue. Wars, for example, or natural disasters, are reduced on the screen to pathetic pictures of refugee women and wounded children. There are comparatively few facts; we are not invited to demand political action or ask questions. We are asked to react with pity and, usually, send money to help. Or, after earthquakes, say, we are informed about efforts by governments or charities to bring in food and shelter for the victims: we are intended to feel cheered that the problems are being 'solved' and we can move on.

Reporters today are not on the scene to inform, they are there to tell us how to *feel*. To that end they seem increasingly to be chosen so that their appearance and ability to show 'empathy' have become a priority in their employment brief. This even includes a growing tendency for anyone reporting tragedy live to be seen on television wringing their hands. The suspicion even crosses my mind that so many news-readers and reporters who tell us sad stories have strong Scottish or Northern Irish accents because their vowel sounds make them sound more anguished than, say, dialects from Yorkshire or the west country, which have more robust consonants. But that is probably fanciful.

The demand for emotional communication, though, does help to explain the number of attractive young women reporters on television required to do little more than look anguished in order to 'project' the essence of the story they are covering on screen. Or smile encouragingly at the antics of cute animals or babies intended to lighten the public mood.

Basically it seems easier for women viewers to empathise with other women as victims than in any other familiar female role – such as bosses, teachers, business women. This applies even when the image of victims' suffering is no more than a means of communication. One example of this was the coverage of the 2004 hostage crisis at a school in Beslan, in southern Russia. On the BBC, a woman reporter stood in an area outside the school. She explained that the 'authorities' would let the TV crew go no further. She stood and talked about what it must feel like to be inside with the 777 children who were taken hostage by Chechen guerrillas; on ITV, a seasoned journalist, Julian Manyon, was inside the building with his cameraman giving us the live experience of what was happening and what it felt like to be there.

This may seem harsh, when there are some superb female reporters doing a highly professional job. Not many of them cover everyday life in Britain, though; they are often those based abroad, outside the feelgood remit. So is it fanciful to suggest that television producers in this country often use women reporters who are apparently chosen for their looks as a way of distracting viewers from the more disastrous implications of a story? In fact, this crowd-pleasing technique was first noticeable in the public-relations industry back in the Eighties, when industries with a problematical public profile – like the nuclear power industry – tended to use pretty women to represent the company and put unpopular points of view. For a start, few men find it easy to be deliberately rude or aggressive to a good-looking young woman, even if she is fudging the facts. Women interviewers, too, tend not to want to seem to be bullying other women, and give the pretty girls an easy ride. This would not apply to women interviewing men.

What is not fanciful is that histrionics of this sort in news coverage do blur reasoned judgement of reality and also limit the scope of truth. The ordinary people John Birt wanted to tell the story necessarily see a very narrow and subjective version of the whole truth and the wider picture. And this does not apply only to television. In the Seventies reporters on the old *Daily Mirror* went out on human-interest stories with photographers, and not the other way round. 'The picture tells the story, you're there to get the names and ages,' young reporters were told. Now too, newspapers and magazines increasingly illustrate coverage of important stories with portraits of the writer, forcing a personal relationship on the reader – which is yet another way to look the wrong way down a telescope.

These devices are part of popular culture's process of reducing the impact of panic or despair, but in effect this manages to distance us from reality because it provides only an illusion of the truth. Remember, during the 9/11 2001 attacks on New York's twin towers, how many witnesses found it hard to recognise the horror of what they were themselves involved in except in terms of oft-repeated disaster movies like *The Towering Inferno* or a *Die Hard* action film. Real life was absorbed by fiction. We can only speculate how far public reaction to George Bush's and Tony Blair's political actions then were coloured by a mass perception that they were 'saviours' cast in the roles of a Steve McQueen or a Bruce Willis. One specific effect in the aftermath was certainly that as popular-culture-style heroes, these politicians could bypass the process of democracy in parliamentary debate, or even votes of Congress.

Whichever way you look at it, it's a moot point whether government has become a tool of popular culture, or popular culture an instrument of government. The effect on public perception is the same. The power of mass media now plays an active political role in government. It has become a kind of interpreter of popular culture's take on what ordinary women, at least, want. The media message may be a cosmic truth -– War is Suffering, for example – but in real terms this is a platitude with hardly any useful part to play in a democratic system of making real decisions about real problems. We are being offered the Truth, but not the Whole Truth, and certainly not Nothing but the Truth.

14

We're dealing with a powerful force here.

For good or ill, the feminised and anti-rational slant of popular culture's moral dimension will dominate aspects of government with much more force than the impact made by women in Parliament, women judges, women administrators, or even a woman Home Secretary.

Popular culture is now using the power base of women's amalgamated political clout for propaganda purposes. It appears to pass without notice that this could be dangerous in the context of society as a whole. It has already paid dividends in the guise of 'weight of popular opinion' to change the operation of the law – as in the Sara Thornton case.

Sara Thornton was sentenced to life in 1990 for killing her husband, whom she described as abusive. Her case was taken up by a powerful lobby of women who wanted to reform the law on domestic violence. The mass media carried out a high-profile campaign supporting her. In 1996 the sentence was commuted to five years' imprisonment for manslaughter and she was released on the grounds of diminished responsibility.

In the Sara Thornton case, a women's lobby using popular culture to wield political power forced an appeal hearing in a case which would probably otherwise have caused little stir on the basis of alleged but legally unsubstantiated domestic violence.

Another example of women using the power popular

culture has given them to bend the rules of the male-orientated system was the case of the British Aerospace plane-wreckers in the 1980s. These women caused criminal damage to aircraft in protest at what they saw as unfair discrimination in the workplace. The damage was undisputed and they did not deny it. But the judge let them off punishment 'because they felt so strongly'.

There are countless examples, too, where sympathy with women or child victims prejudges a case against an accused man. The Rachel Nickell case, for one; and also the murder of the TV presenter Jill Dando. In such cases, the mass media provide only grudging acknowledgment of the wrong done to innocent men wrongly jailed with its vociferous encouragement. Now, it seems that the government wants to make the pain of victims' relatives a factor in sentencing. The mind boggles at the opportunities this will provide for the mass media to galvanise emotions.

Ordinary women as a political force are increasingly using mass-cultural outlets to become society's watchdogs and behavioural police. Various punitive authorities – the benefits system, the charities against abuse of children, the police, for example – depend on and encourage people to spy on each other and report people they think suspicious. We have seen innocent paediatricians attacked by mothers who assume that they are paedophiles. This is seen as regrettable, no doubt, but few women would say they didn't understand how it happened. The danger is that at one end of the scale malicious prejudice, and at the other emotional sympathy for criminals' excuses for their actions, might become the basis for punishment or exoneration, rather than evidence and proof.

Simply, in order to feed public hunger for drama and

sensation, the mass media plays on emotion and indignation. The public responds by making monsters out of those they are encouraged to hate and blame.

The case of Maxine Carr, the girlfriend of Soham murderer Ian Huntley, illustrates this. She was away from home when the murders happened, but she did lie to give Huntley an alibi. When she was tried for perverting the course of justice, the court accepted that she had lied because she genuinely believed in his innocence. She was sentenced to three and a half years in jail. It's hard to pretend that the monstrous level of Huntley's crime was not so appalling that it almost put him beyond the scope of media hatred and disgust. The crime was so inhuman that popular culture could not bring it within its own bounds of sensation and shock. But people needed the catharsis of having someone to blame, they needed someone ordinary so they knew who they were hating. This was Maxine Carr. Yet what she did is done to a small degree by hundreds of women every year when they think their husbands or partners are wrongly accused, and they do not become public pariahs.

For good or ill, women as a political force are increasingly using mass popular cultural outlets to rewrite basic justice as enshrined in law. And some women are not above using to their own advantage the mass media's lack of definition about what is true and what is emotional preconception.

This applies to the case of Karen Matthews, the mother who arranged her own daughter's disappearance to obtain money from the media. Ms Matthews used every popular-culture trick in the book to inspire sympathy and public support when she reported her nine-year-old daughter Shannon as missing. Her actions, it seems, were a perverted attention-seeking, or money-grubbing – or both – manipulation of the coverage of the disappearance of Madeleine McCann in Portugal. Karen Matthews even tried to copy the powerful mass-media image of the grieving mother carrying the missing child's toy which had attracted massive public sympathy for Kate McCann. In Karen Matthews' case, even when Shannon's disappearance seemed genuine, the contrast would have been comic if it had not been grotesque.

There were no moral nuances in the media coverage, however. At first the tabloids and television did their best to create Karen Matthews as a tragic-victim heroine. But she became a monster overnight when it emerged that she had planned the abduction of her child to make money by selling her story to a newspaper. The mass media turned on her. Her boyfriend was charged with pornography offences. Her sex life was dredged through and condemned. Her friends talked about the way she had betrayed them. She was jailed for kidnap – which begs the question of whether a mother can, technically, kidnap her own child.

But in the end it seemed as though the people hated her most for playing popular culture to sucker them. Friends and family spoke of their feelings of betrayal because they had wasted their sympathy on her. If anyone in the media ever asked what happened to the child, Shannon, or to Karen's other children, after their mother was jailed, I missed it.

Perhaps this is popular culture's version of seeing justice done; perhaps it involves nothing more than a shift of judgmental style, not a sinister moral manipulation of innocent people. That might be argued as long as there are institutions which still adhere to fixed standards of truth-telling to retain public trust. Like the BBC, surely?

On February 3rd 2009, there was a chilling moment on the BBC1 *Breakfast* programme. The previous day had seen traffic chaos due to snow. Schools were closed, hospitals calling for workers to get to work if they could as they were short-staffed because of the weather. Small businesses were apparently losing millions of pounds by the hour. The presenters had asked viewers to send in their pictures of the snow.

What's wrong with that? Thirty-five thousand pictures of snow were sent electronically to the BBC. On the 3rd, the programme presenter interviewed a nice girl called 'an interactive reporter'. Yes, the response had been a record. The presenter said in passing that this told us something about the public participation in journalism, and the interactive reporter agreed. Quite often, she said, the public delivered news pictures before the BBC cameramen could provide them.

Maybe there is nothing wrong with that. It's a very harmless case to argue from, anyway. But in a way, that is the point. This was a tiny instance, when the public actually provided 'facts' which were broadcast without question and accepted by the public as news. But what of the implications for coverage of more significant circumstances? Where does the process of the viewers supplying factual news stop? Because by definition that news is subjective, not objective. Would actual misrepresentation, too, pass unremarked? That small item on the programme was evidence – which should surely be alarming – that members of the public can create and broadcast on the 'official' news channel their own highly subjective version of fact without any process of objective filtering for bias or simple lying.

At the very least, there's the question of how far news

providers will go in letting their viewers take over the provision of news. Of course there are times when onlookers see something – a plane crash, perhaps – which television or newspapers cannot reach immediately, and the immediacy of their words and pictures provides valuable impact. But in these days of cost-cutting, there is a real danger that the job of gathering news will be left to a new, more dangerous version of what used to be called ambulance-chasers. It's one thing if they do it for money; it is much more significant if they are motivated by ideology or exploitation.

Popular culture in any form has to make its point at once or it won't at all. In practice this means that every issue is reduced to opposing extremes, which provides drama. The middle ground is dull. Compromise is dull. Agreement is dull. Inevitably, to sustain interest demands drama which depends on shock. This drives ever-increasing sensationalism. Which involves perversion of aspects of truth. This can range from distortion and exaggeration to the sort of news management which leaves out what is deemed boring, however essential to the factual truth those boring bits might be.

Wherever popular culture plays any part in decision-making, we risk reducing the real issues to a latter-day Roman circus.

Today in Britain it goes without saying that politicians' battles for electoral support are fought and won by the skill of spin doctors appealing direct on screen or by written word to the emotions of the electorate. Image is paramount – there's a fortune spent on clothes, styling, haircuts, fitness, and that's men as well as women. People in power know already that for the mass of people they reach, the issue is not what they say, but the way that they say it, and how they look when they are saying it. Political power becomes a process of seduction, not persuasion.

We are facing a reality where there is Truth According To Popular Culture and there is Factual Truth. Already on the BBC and ITV news, for example, and in the tabloid press, factual truth often comes a poor second. And everyone who depends on any kind of public support – politicians, employers, administrators, the police – knows which truth counts.

This has a bearing on what we are not told as well as how we are told it. It's easy enough to make us feel happy and secure as long as the electorate allows itself to be fobbed off with what the mass media provide.

This process is well established now, and it isn't something we can avoid. News management by the media has become a given. But now popular culture's empowered and feminised constituency shows signs of moving beyond the control of reality or fact.

For a while we may believe that the benefits of prioritising positive emotion over intractable issues could lead to a kinder, saner society. In many ways we probably do live in a more caring, more understanding, more tolerant society than most people did fifty years ago. But not, I think, a more liberated one.

Emotions can be manipulated; without facts, without reason, without knowledge, people in a society are easier to manipulate and control. We have to be aware that the very popular culture which has done so much to free the mass of ordinary women from the traditional stereotypes and expectations which denied them real equality in society has given them access to unaccustomed new power. But it has given them no information or knowledge as to how to use that power in confronting reality.

If, that is, they ever do have to face reality. Popular culture seems to be colonising new technologies as they are developed to make it possible for people to avoid confronting real life altogether. When issues are reduced to a state of feeling – fear, or outrage, for example, or pity – merely suffering such emotion is presented as tantamount to taking action to solve the problems.

This can be effective on a political level, as, for instance, with the original Live Aid concerts in aid of the starving in Ethiopia. But even so, the impact of the concerts themselves inevitably transcended the issue of suffering, in spite of Bob Geldof's efforts to prevent just that.

Some will ask, Does it matter? Some sort of news management is inevitable, simply at the level of choosing what makes a news story and what does not. A problem does arise when the news is managed by government to bring about a specific reaction from the public in the interests of that government. That is the mark of totalitarianism and it signals the end of free speech and of liberal thought in our society. Or any thought at all, if popular culture has its way.

It is an insidious process, designed, no doubt, for our own good. Does it matter that on 12th February, Sir James Crosby, deputy chairman of the City watchdog, the Financial Services Authority – and previously chief executive of HBOS, one of the banks which had to be rescued by the government – resigned minutes before Prime Minister Gordon Brown was to face a grilling in the House of Commons at Prime Minister's Questions about his personal appointment to the FSA of Sir James, a man implicated in the sacking of a whistle-blower at HBOS, who had warned as far back as 2004 that the bank was expanding too quickly.

What the Crosby resignation did was to deflect any hostile questions which would have dented the Prime Minister's credibility. Because of the timing of the resignation, the question of the Prime Minister's judgement was never raised in Parliament. The public was not being served then.

Does it matter that the same week a member of the staff at Conservative Central Office made an amendment to the on-line encyclopaedia Wikipedia 'correcting' the date of birth of the painter Titian because shortly before the Tory leader David Cameron had accused Gordon Brown in the House of getting it wrong when he had not?

Yes it does, because it creates evidence of deliberate deceit. And it shows the total lack of respect which society's leaders show towards the ordinary people who must live under their control.

These examples of overt manipulation of government and of the public may be trivial in themselves, but cumulatively they utterly undermine people's confidence that what is seen and said in the mass media or by government can be trusted.

Such doctoring of information is an important element of the way the mass media deliberately engineers a public response. For example, the world faced a very real threat of nuclear war between India and Pakistan over Kashmir. The future of millions of people hung in the balance. But the main item on the BBC TV news was the announcement of the birth of a baby to the then Chancellor of the Exchequer, Gordon Brown. The real threat of nuclear war came second to that. Popular culture's message came over loud and clear to millions of ordinary women: The world may be about to fall apart, but here in Britain we can still feel good about the miracle of birth. Dream on.

15

The effects of women's political empowerment on the mass media is a crucial factor in considering where society is now headed. It is important to investigate the trivial and perverse nature of the power that ordinary women now have to influence the way we are governed.

Of course, government pretends to believe itself to be directing the people's lives. But would MPs have to try so painfully hard to curry favour with the public in the guise of media celebrities if this were really so?

In fact, popular culture acts as sole interpreter of changing, subjective facets of what pleases the ordinary women consumers who keep the economy afloat, and the government acts accordingly. Basically, the priority of any party politician is to get re-elected, so few MPs dare do anything else.

I should say before we go any further that in the context of this book government covers the whole panoply of parliamentary administration rather than simply the government in power. Whichever party is in power, the mass media and the governmental structure are mutually dependent, mutually supportive – and mutually exclusive of outside authority. Except, it has to be said, from the influence of popular culture's media moguls, men like Rupert Murdoch who can use the power vested in them by popular culture to influence government.

At ground level, though, popular culture is aimed implicitly at the powerless. It gathers the weakest in society – the poor, the confused, all the lowest common denominators – and unites them at a level from which no one is excluded. This works to unite ordinary women in particular because they have been conditioned historically to see themselves as victims. And in keeping with that conditioning, the process involves little reciprocal effort, no knowledge, no education, no effort of the mind.

True, popular culture has probably gone well beyond what was originally intended in the degree of empowerment it has given the mass of women. But this is what it has done, and so, as a mass, these women are no longer powerless. However, their symbiotic relationship with popular culture has given them no real-life experience of any alternative mode of exercising this power. Ordinary women who partake of this sort of power have consequently cut themselves off, in effect, from the ability to act outside the norms laid down by popular culture.

The women politicised by popular culture are powerful by weight of numbers. Their power has nothing to do with them as individual people. Once an individual tries to operate politically outside this mass, she loses access to the amalgam of female power and is at once rendered insignificant and powerless.

Also, because women as a group protect that group against anything and anyone who threatens its strength-in-numbers, the individual who questions the operation of the group becomes its enemy, an outcast, and a traitor to her sex. So the interests of the mass will always prevail.

There might have been a way out of this political cul-de-sac if enough British women were the change-agents that Dr Christine de Panafieu cited in her EU research study as vital to social progress. Had such women existed in Britain, they might have been able to alter the fundamental social and psychological framework under which society operates.

But this did not happen. Nor were the women who became politically important the feminist activists who actually set out to bring about that change because they were opposed to the male-orientated status quo. Instead they were the ordinary women content to leave the structure as it was and merely tinker with the details to their own advantage.

As a result many women still operate on the assumption that they are ultimately dependent. They may be aware that men cannot and do not now automatically fulfil the protective role, but women have no great incentive to stand out from their female group to take on a hierarchical responsibility for others. They want to be looked after. That is, they are prepared to behave like old-style traditional women as the nurturers, and to play the supportive role to other women, but they do this within a carefully defined structure where women do not lead, they act in unison under the control of an outside statutory authority or system.

That control is now exercised by government. As we have seen, however, government has been reconstituted as part of popular culture's dialogue with its consumers.

Given that ordinary women look to government as stand-in for the social role originally played within the family by men, they expect government instead to deal with them according to the traditional definitions of the old, established concepts of femininity.

Increasingly we have seen government take on the paterfamilias role, laying down the guidelines by which mothers and wives and family nurturers should carry out their feminine role. All for their own good, no doubt, but this process gradually erodes women's individual ability to act outside the guidelines without appearing to neglect their female duty to home and family, and consequently failing in their feminine function.

These government strictures have included limits on punishment of children; what to eat and drink and smoke without endangering a foetus; health, and what is safe to drink and eat; controlling what children watch on TV, or deciding when they first taste alcohol . . . the list goes on and on. In short, women have allowed government to take on a controlling role in the personal and private area which was once where they were able to make their own decisions.

But perhaps it would be a mistake to put this down to a growing fascist tendency in popular culture/government. Maybe it is a side-effect of a well-intentioned political policy. After all, the mass media is making provision for new forms of democratic input so that people can think that they participate in the way they are controlled.

There has never been greater opportunity for ordinary people to have their say by e-mailing or texting their comments in response to what they are watching on television or hearing on radio. And it's hard to suppress the anxiety, when watching, say, morning television, that once a few e-mails have been read out expressing subjective agreement or disagreement with a point made, that is tantamount, in the minds of the programme's producers and presenters, to balanced judgement of an issue.

When viewers are asked to e-mail their questions before an interview with the Home Secretary or the Chancellor of the Exchequer, having to re-present the resultant list of predictably personal concerns sent in for answer exonerates the interviewer from having to give the policy-maker a grilling with questions which cannot be answered with a glib sound-bite. Thus in the end it is the viewers who collude in being patronised or protected from unpalatable truth.

This process apparently translates in people's perception to the belief that they are participating in the democratic process. They are 'having their say'. And too often they are satisfied with that. To judge by the questions they want answered, the public shows little interest in probing for the truth, or for questioning what the mass media tells them. Too often it seems that they want politicians to be able to answer the easy questions they ask because it makes women, in particular, feel confident that someone knows what they're doing. Seeing someone who is an integral part of the massive guardian that is the state made to flounder and look incompetent causes public dismay and doubt. Women want to feel confident that someone or something is in control.

Popular culture is constantly demonstrating that most people do not want excellence and professionalism. They find high quality intimidating. Take TV shows like *Strictly Come Dancing* or the *X Factor*, or *Dancing on Ice*, where the public vote can make nonsense of the scoring of professional judges. Time after time millions who phone in to support their 'favourite' performer vote for the least skilful, the one the expert judges dismiss.

This became a subject for TV magazine-show debate in 2008 when neo-celebrity John Sergeant, a dancing no-hoper, was 'saved' week after week by the public vote on *Strictly Come Dancing*. The indignant judges appeared on news and discussion programmes to protest that Mr

Sergeant, a retired political journalist, had no dancing skill and did not improve. *Strictly Come Dancing*, they argued, was a dance contest and he could not dance. They objected that he survived in the competition at the expense of 'better' contestants who were eliminated instead. The point that the judges never appreciated was that the public loved their bumbling hero because he was bad. His clumsy efforts were entertaining and loveable while the skilful did not engage the public's affections.

In the end, Mr Sergeant did the decent thing and quit the programme, saying he was worried that he might win if he stayed.

It seems absurd to take this seriously. It is, however, just one example of the low-level standards of skill or ability demanded by popular culture. In all these talent shows, when experts criticise the lack of talent of a performer the members of the public have taken to their hearts, the audience boos the critic, not the contestant. Unsuccessful candidates on *The X-Factor* or *Dragons' Den* rarely look to themselves for reasons for their failure. They abuse the judges, or plead with the wider television audience. They don't just reject criticism, they don't believe it. They are convinced the critics are lying – usually because they are 'jealous'.

Popular culture does not teach us to appreciate quality or skill; it promotes the clown or the freak, anyone who makes the most direct appeal to the emotions. It devalues expertise and professionalism because they preclude the excitement and sensation of dramatic failure.

This last point can be illustrated by a series of TV talent contests where composer Andrew Lloyd Webber presided over singing contests to pick stars for musicals he was to produce in the West End. The lead part in *The Sound of Music* and the role of Nancy in *Oliver Twist* were allocated in this way.

The implications of this for professional singers who had trained for years for just such a role were ignored; in fact the casting vote system which seems to allow the public to choose their own stars appears to have generated more trade for the musicals concerned when they come to the stage, as audiences flock to see proof that popular culture does deliver on the dream. Part of that dream is that everyone could be a celebrity.

What we should ask ourselves is whether this self-promoting bravado on the part of the viewing public is masking some kind of mass inferiority complex whenever people have to confront reality. If the public set their own cultural standards low, that suggests people see that low level as the value of their own satisfaction. That has broader implications for society as a whole where it would appear to suggest that for a considerable number of ordinary people, assiduous training and practice may actually be counter-productive.

Some years ago, I remember talking to a worker at the Ford factory at Halewood on Merseyside. He had worked hard for promotion to foreman and was proud to get the job. But then things started to happen. His tools mysteriously disappeared, or he found them broken. His workmates avoided him; he was left out of rounds in the pub after work; his former friends no longer shared their jokes with him. He was excluded from the camaraderie which had made him enjoy working at the factory, and in the end he gave up the foreman's job.

'They didn't like it because they thought I was pushing

myself forward and thought I was better than them,' he said.

It was the same syndrome as in all those TV police series where, if there's a 'toff' in the cast, he or she is inevitably the villain. Too often, those who are perceived to be rejecting the lowest standards and trying to improve themselves are seen as doing so at the expense of those weaker than themselves and therefore they are hostile to the majority.

This attitude was illustrated in the mass media in the final stages of 2009's BBC TV's *University Challenge*. Gail Trimble, a post-graduate student and the captain of the winning team from Corpus Christi College, Oxford, gave several stunning performances to ensure victory for her college. Over the series, she personally amassed 825 of the 1,235 points won by Corpus Christi. There was speculation that she might be the cleverest student ever to appear on the contest.

But Ms Trimble's was not a popular-culture image. The public tried to drag her down to the level popular culture can deal with. 'She has become the new public pariah,' wrote the *Daily Mail.* Instead of celebration, she was subjected to abuse and insults in both the tabloids and on the Internet; and the dislike she stirred seems to have been purely on the grounds that she did not need popular culture to empower her. 'A hateful know-all'; 'a horse-toothed snob . . . '; 'brain-rupturingly irritating . . . ', wrote the bloggers.

This rather long-winded argument is leading to a simple assertion. Popular culture has brought us to the point that we choose the men and women we look up to – the people who govern us – very much on the basis of the popular voter on a TV talent show. We seem to discount specialist knowledge and dedication in favour of charismatic popular-culture celebrities. So Ben Elton becomes a best-selling novelist; pop singer Bono becomes a statesman; Ginger Spice becomes Geri Halliwell, United Nations special envoy; Boris Johnson becomes Mayor of London.

Yes, it's new blood. But we are in a Catch-22 bind. Government directs what the public should and shouldn't do. But government bases its policies on what it thinks a very significant section of the electorate (ordinary women) want it to do; it acts to please the greatest number in its desperation to be liked, so in effect it is not initiating policy and leading from the front; it is following the mass media, that echo of the voices of ordinary women. Ergo, like a dog chasing its tail, there can be no progress outside the circle.

Such a scenario means that fundamentally the social system cannot progress. Ordinary women do not want social change because what exists already protects their interests. There is no subversive will amongst ordinary women to destroy that. Revolution is not in popular culture's remit.

Women are caught in a vicious circle; they have escaped from domestic oppression only to find they have nothing tangible to replace it. They have tried to improve their experience of their own lives, and have indeed done so. But in the end it is tinkering with the details of something already established. Society as a whole needs to move on, but there's a dearth of ideas and action to facilitate this. Popular culture itself reflects this staleness. Much that is called 'new' in fashion and pop music now is actually retrospective.

The question is where the women politically empowered

by popular culture can go now. The feminist writer Dale Spender wrote in her 1984 book, *Time and Tide Wait For No Man*, that 'There are news items, articles, even books, beginning to suggest with increased frequency that the current women's movement is wavering and that some of these women have overlooked the positive features of home and are advised to go back and resample some of its simple pleasures.'

Today, indeed, popular culture seems to be recycling the same old concepts. Ads are back on TV about women wanting whiter whites and fresher-smelling homes, or taking credit for cooking meals they actually heated in the microwave.

But if ordinary women are looking back to adapt traditional femininity to current popular culture, that old definition of femininity is different now. Women show little interest in pleasing men per se, not husbands, anyway; domestic achievement usually seems to be in spite of them. It no longer entails domestic skills or practice, only ready-cooked meals and the microwave. Popular culture has made even domesticity into conspicuous consumption and an opportunity for women to project an image of themselves. Domesticity is part of the fashionable expression of self; it is nothing to do with the old concept of femininity, looking after others. Specifically men.

Forms of popular culture, like television sitcoms and soaps, or the advertisements which now sponsor as well as interrupt mass-audience programmes, now almost invariably show women in charge at home, and frequently at work, too.

This may well reflect what has happened in society, but there are signs that ordinary women are tending to turn backwards in their outlook rather than forwards to the unknown. It is as though they are looking to popular culture, on television, in music, in fashion and in advertising, for reruns of the old familiar images and messages that once empowered them.

It seems that ordinary women are afraid of the future which popular culture now offers them.

It is as though they like where they are – or rather, where they were in their own popular culture prime – and have had enough of change. So self-help books are no longer telling women how to break through the glass ceiling, they're telling them that they will get stress illnesses if they do. The media quotes with approval a research report from the Children's Society that working mothers' selfishness in pursuing their own interests is damaging their children. Interestingly, these children were described on television as 'the most precious *commodity* we have'. Popular culture, you see, knows which side its bread is buttered! Children are apparently already included in the public mind as part of a constituent market group.

What it comes down to is that the major political issues of the day – about mothers staying at home, about women's working hours, about the role of fathers – all sound like retro debates from the 1960s. Ordinary women, just as the feminists did in the Seventies and Eighties, are simply staying put in political terms, and digging themselves a hole to hide in.

There is a reason for this. Popular culture in all its traditional forms is itself losing the source of its own ability to empower. The mass media and government together seem to be teetering on the brink of impotence.

16

If women are beginning to fear their own inability to control society through popular culture, there must be doubt about the performance of government itself.

It is the way the feminine-orientated priorities and characteristics of popular culture have permeated legislative and decision-making processes in society that is questionable. Anyone who doubts this should note the words of what amounted to a statement of intent on 1st March 2009 from Harriet Harman, Deputy Leader of the Labour Party and Minister for Women and Equality.

It had been announced that the Royal Bank of Scotland, which had recently had to be rescued by taxpayers' money, was to pay its former Chief Executive, fifty-year-old Sir Fred Goodwin, a pension of £693,000 a year.

Harriet Harman revealed the extent of government's capitulation to mass culture, and the erosion of the rule of law, in her comment on Prime Minister Gordon Brown's avowed intention to claw back the money paid to Sir Fred for the state. She said on television: 'It might be enforceable in a court of law, this contract, but it's not enforceable in the court of public opinion and that's where the Government steps in.'

No doubt Ms Harman intended to assert the government's determination to act in response to the emotional pressure of outraged public opinion. What she did was to provide proof positive of the way government is reneging on its proper function – to govern within the law – in favour of pleasing public opinion.

The mass of ordinary women, however outraged they may be about Sir Fred's pension, will be alarmed, not placated, by such evidence that the government is so overtly helpless to lead. That is not what these women ever looked for. What they have always wanted is that government – or parents, or husbands, or teachers, or lawyers or doctors or some faceless bureaucrat – should take responsibility for the consequences of their emotions.

We have said that it is the political empowerment of ordinary women, as part of the process of popular culture's indoctrination of the female psyche, which has contributed hugely to the nature of that feminine takeover of the once male-orientated system. Many men as well as women would welcome this as a chance for a fresh approach. If there is a concern, though, it has to lie, first, in the narrow range that popular culture imposes on the women it empowers; and, second, in where their priorities are concentrated.

There is a limit to the popular culture's areas of interest – usually associated with its commercial scope. Over the last decade or so there has been an overt political concentration, where the electorate demands that government respond to public pressure, on 'soft' or female areas like health, personal spending, and education.

The mass media decides where this political concentration fixes attention, but popular culture is easily satisfied by promises of intent – perhaps an inquiry, or more research, or simply 'We'll look into it'. There is no requirement at all for vision or action, which is too long-term for the political expediency demanded by the media.

Also, a feminised society has different priorities from the old male-orientated systems. There has been a deliberate steering away from competitiveness, celebration of individual success, or personal ambition, and a move towards team spirit, family values, and the greater good of the greatest number. Basically, the whole concept of meritocracy is dead. This gives women a sense of security because they are not going to be found wanting. It is part of the security blanket of a feminised society to be amongst the ordinary majority where there is safety in numbers.

All forms of popular culture have collaborated to foster among women in particular a fear of being unsupported. This applies as much to being without a man or without friends as it does to doing or thinking or looking different from the crowd. Popular culture has always manipulated this fear, a form of the herd mentality, which seems to be instinctive in any mass group of women. It is a fear cultivated by the mass media to hold consumers' attention. This may help to explain the increasing levels of bullying in schools and institutions and even offices during the decades of popular culture's growth of influence. To protect itself, any group where weakness is masked by strength of numbers wants to destroy the one who stands out against it.

When the female-biased priorities of popular culture actually operate unchallenged as part of government, which is what Tony Blair brought about, then questions arise about the quality of that government as it is delivered to the end-users, the public. Can government operate if no one dares stand out to test it?

In theory, the public can take action in their own defence at the ballot box. In practice, though, this sanction is less effective when all parties see an overriding necessity to pander to popular culture's promotion of politicians as creatures of the mass media. The demands of the mass media compel politicians not to lead, but to react to majority public opinion. That tends to blur policy differences between parties, and limit the range of choice.

No doubt aiming to please, government has reduced decision-making to a kind of sound-bite method of law-making and social control. In practice, the decisions the government makes, on behalf of the electorate in a social system which is now patently female-orientated, are invariably imposed in a populist and arbitrary way in reaction to a degree of public hysteria. There is no effective public consultation or consideration of how bad the legislation is as workable law.

For example, after eight-year-old Sarah Payne was murdered in July 2000 and a previously convicted paedo-phile was later found guilty of killing her, the *News of the World* ran a campaign for new legislation which would allow mothers access to the names of men on the Sex Offenders Register who might be living or working near their homes. In 2008, a Sarah's Law pilot scheme was launched in four areas of the country. This allows mothers to register with police their concerns about, say, a new partner, or a neighbour. The police will then check and warn the mother if the man has any previous conviction as a sex offender. No doubt they will err on the safe side, hence it is written into the law: 'Those mothers who fail to keep any information they are given to themselves could be prosecuted.'

Home Secretary Jacqui Smith called these pilot schemes 'a huge step forward'. She said, 'I want to see every child living their lives free from fear.'

She seemed blind to the wider potential consequences for innocent citizens, showing no concern about the scope for malice, for mistakes, or for the effect on men who have never abused a child but might be on the Sex Offenders Register because they slept with a fifteen-year-old girl who lied that she was older; or a man who urinated in public and was on the Register for indecent exposure. Ms Smith seemed to ignore the proven workings of Megan's Law, a similar piece of ill-conceived legislation in the USA, which had already resulted in actual vigilante killings, and in the hounding of innocent men because of mistaken identity. It had also driven some sex offenders underground, thus defeating the object of the exercise.

The point here is not the necessity of making children safe from attack; it is about the consequences of government's knee-jerk and imperfect legislative reaction to mass-media manipulation of an overwhelming pressure from emotional public demands for action. In introducing laws and regulations based on hysterical pressure and the mass media, the government has actually distorted the concept of justice. The way popular culture interprets justice 'justifies' the mobs of mothers who have attacked men released into the community after serving their sentences when news leaked that they are on the Sex Offenders Register.

When the judiciary and the justice system was able to operate independently of politics, there was a strong cerebral element to its administration and a degree of faith that it was not corrupt. It was the one powerful protection society had from the incursions of mass-media-led, one-off, emotional pressure-group interests. Government populist law-making (like allowing a victim's family a right to a say in sentencing those who committed the offence) undermines that protection of objectivity.

The government is no longer convincing empowered

women that it is providing them with the protection and support that they, the mainstay of the electorate, crave. At all levels of our feminised society, in vast numbers, we have allowed ourselves to become dependent on the state. Reliance on popular culture to create the self-images we aspire to has eroded our sense of personal responsibility for what we are and do. And any sense of guilt about what we may have done. At one stage, perhaps, women looking for the backup and protection they had once expected from men were looking for no more than a notional gesture of support from government. Now the need to feel cared for has become a form of comfort-addiction, like eating junk food or binge drinking.

This psychological dependence on government may work in an economic boom and as long as popular culture is able to flourish by expanding its commercial interests into pastures new. Come a bust, though, and the inability of government to repair the system comes to light.

Some will protest that the cracks in the fabric of society were beginning to show in Britain decades ago, and they are right. The general public, though, were not aware of it. Nor, apparently, was government. The gulf that increasingly loomed in the public mind between reality and the virtual dreamworld that the mass media created has masked what was really happening. The public, particularly women who wanted to live the dream, did not want to stop and think what they were doing. And when the system of government is actually implicated in the dreamworld, where can ordinary people learn the 'real' truth. Indeed, what is real?

For years, for example, ordinary women's fears have been growing about the threat of crime, and the dangers of becoming a victim of crime. Television series like *The Bill*, soaps like *EastEnders*, magazines telling the real-life experiences of crime victims; ever more violent crime novels; newspaper campaigns on behalf of the victims of crime, or against carrying knives or guns, all combine to create an underlying atmosphere of imminent threat.

Official statistics paint a different picture. Government figures contradict the evidence of our own fears. Violent crime, they insist, is going down, there are more police on the streets, women are safe to go out.

Which is the truth?

Both versions may be true. The fear of crime is absolutely real to the women who now feel they can't go out alone at night into a town centre to the cinema or a restaurant. Their fears are so real to them that it limits their freedom and curtails their lives so as not to put themselves in the way of danger. No statistical evidence will convince them otherwise. That is their perception of the truth, so, in effect, it becomes true.

These women do not trust the Home Office figures which contradict their fears. The truth that matters to those women is the perception, not the facts. That's what affects the way they live their lives. That's what is real to them. They believe that government is not addressing their real problems. Thus government increasingly appears irrelevant to real life.

Frankly, has our system of government become inadequate? Is it even fit for purpose?

Before I try to explain the basis for raising such a claim, I would like to mention a few of the grounds for making it.

A democratic government, whichever political party forms it, represents the electorate as a whole. Of course the colour of the party in power is bound to affect the slant of policy-making in favour of one social sector or another, but even in the kind of three-line-whip-powered committee dictatorships the two-party system tends to create in this country, it is important that members of government take a broader view than they would normally as party politicians.

We have examined in some detail in previous chapters why the attitudes and priorities of the electorate today have changed significantly since the 1960s. This has been largely a shift towards society's feminine side because of popular culture's dramatic success in turning the mass of ordinary women from passive dependants into an economic and political powerhouse which harnesses the mass media to pursue female interests.

The ways in which popular culture has affected successive generations of the women it has empowered have been adapted and developed in different periods. Popular culture is driven by mass commercial demand, which changes constantly, and the mass media has had to keep expanding in new ways to stimulate continuous spending. Hence the constant reaching for something different from what went before.

Inevitably this process has involved an element of turning each succeeding age group of ordinary women against its predecessors. That is basic marketing methodology, to create new markets out of each generation's desire to be different from the one before. This is crucial to popular culture. Until the Sixties, girls generally dressed in the same clothes as their mothers, and expected to live very similar lives to theirs.

The popular-media-led fashions of the Sixties and Seventies revolutionised the shape of young women's bodies with tights and the mini-skirt; in addition, the new sexual and assertive female role model images changed the prevailing morality and caused young women, en masse, to turn against their mothers' values. Shifts in prevailing moral attitudes are at the heart of the social changes popular culture has brought about.

Outside its own commercial groupings then, popular culture does not unite women. It creates an illusion that it does, though, because ordinary women in their millions watch the same shows, lust after the same pop idols, wear the same clothes. There is a language of popular culture we all speak, rather as English is the 'official', second language of Europe. Women also share the experience of seeing and hearing the same media messages and confronting the same social issues. Whether you call it dumbing down or standardisation, the effect is the same. On the level of popular culture, we share feelings and emotional prejudices, aspirations and images, but beyond its scope, we don't talk to each other; we are not innovative or creative; we don't join together to do and act and think. Not like we used to, anyway. When BBC *Gardeners' World* broadcast an item on city allotments a year or two ago, it was a revelation to the television team when the programme ignited a surge of community spirit and camaraderie. Back-to-basics campaigner and TV chef Hugh Fearnley-Whittingstall also tapped into the same undercurrent of social enthusiasm with his urban food-producing small-holding in Bristol. On both programmes, older people repeated like a call to arms, 'This is more like how it always used to be . . . .'

But, on the whole, the standardised images and the emotional involvements that popular culture provides actually promote a fairly uniform lifestyle which discourages real human contact on any other level. Its hold over the mass mentality of the nation has even broken down barriers of class. Definitions of class had changed anyway after the Second World War, and the divisions became blurred, redrawn rather by money into haves and have-nots, which is how the mass media defines its markets.

Commerce fuels popular culture, of course, but it depends on market growth. Access to it is purely on the grounds of spending power; the dreams it sells have to be universal so as not to restrict demand.

In real daily life, however, we no longer 'know' each other, nor recognise instinctively the common ground within groups. Within generations women are defensive of their own group because it defines them, and those outside that group are outsiders, therefore they do not 'count'. Outsiders are devalued because they don't share the recognition signals which the popular culture of each era provides – catch phrases, exclamations, slogans, things like that. Until, that is, these insiders are overtaken by the next wave of new, young consumer recruits and they, in their turn, become the outsiders.

Popular culture imposes a superficial sameness on its mass consumers, but on a cerebral level also it blurs real distinctions between people.

The stereotypical idiosyncrasies by which people were once able to recognise each other are gone. Miners, for example, 'knew' other miners, they felt safe in making assumptions about the sort of men they were; train drivers understood what made each other tick; farmers recognised themselves in other sons of the soil. They shared a group persona that fostered community and loyalty.

And women had this too. Monstrous regiment or no, women understood each other only too well until the workings of popular culture drove a wedge between them. The Colonel's Lady and Rosie O'Grady were sisters under the skin. They shared basic norms that were accepted as female givens.

But women don't know who they are any more. For the fifty years during which they have been empowered to explore their own potential outside the domestic housewife-and-mother cage, they have tried to define themselves through the changing phases of popular culture. But ultimately popular culture's definitions have served to confuse. They are like chocolate, sweet and briefly satisfying, but essentially it is fleeting because popular culture cannot be anything but superficial, distorting, and psychologically one-dimensional, and life is not like that. Popular culture has taken women to a point where they have political power, but the nature of their power is ephemeral and without solid foundation, and they don't understand it anyway.

Which is where we come back to the question of whether government in this country is fit for purpose.

Before popular culture, government took for granted certain traditional givens about the female sex, that they were primarily wives and mothers and, even if they worked, instinctively put home and family first. As far as pre-popular-culture government had been concerned, that blanket definition covered all ages and all types of women. Divergence between generations of women within that inclusive blueprint made no impression on political policy-making.

But since the Sixties, such a catch-all definition has become actively offensive to women themselves. There has been considerable fragmentation within the female sex as a whole. Government has failed to keep pace with the way these different generations define themselves as disparate from other women. Even in political philosophy these days, there is no such thing as a typical woman, a typical mother, a typical granny.

As long as women kept the economy booming, there was no problem, because the female power base and government shared common goals.

But economic collapse is bound to erode the political dominance of the women whom popular culture empowered, which depended on their spending. Growing unemployment, huge personal debt, and lack of money to spend are increasingly making demands on a mass of women which they cannot meet. Without the power to spend freely, they will lose the basis of their influence.

However, ordinary women have got used to the feeling of being politically powerful as spenders. Popular culture has made certain that most women feel deserving of the cumulative power they have. These women are not yet fully aware that because what they feel they deserve is based on continued commercial expansion, it is now under serious threat. They assume that popular culture (in this case the government) will find solutions.

Still, women continue to operate as emotional pressure groups, not an electorate. The government meanwhile appears to play up its popular-culture credentials. Politicians, of course, constantly claim to be in touch with the common people. They assume that sharing the same popular culture will bring this about. They appear on popular television programmes like *Have I Got News For You*, or make guest appearances on TV soaps, as did Charles Kennedy when

Liberal Democrat leader in a 2004 Christmas episode of *EastEnders*, or Harold Wilson, when Prime Minister, in the *Morecambe and Wise* show; they even leap at the chance to make fools of themselves on celebrity reality shows. Peter Mandelson, the Secretary for Business, let it be known, as soon as he was recalled to government, that he would like to be invited to take part in *Strictly Come Dancing*. Members of Parliament used to play up working-class roots as Men of the People; now they want to be classless mass-media celebrities to give them popular-culture credentials.

However, for ordinary people the reality is now something else. In a recession real people have to live, eat, and earn in a grossly overcrowded society which demands institutional frameworks of regulation or law and order. If the public perception is that these have become inadequate to people's needs, those people lose confidence in the system.

The 2009 economic recession has highlighted how important this is. Few would argue that where the electorate judge the government, through the mass media, their perception is that it is no longer in control of events. The television performances of government spokesmen and women make this obvious as they repeat defensive and meaningless mantras. They announce rescue policies which they cannot enforce. They blame foreigners and refuse to reveal truths. Most of all, as the by-product of popular culture that government now is, they typically display no sense of being prepared to take responsibility for anything that happens.

This must be perceived as a betrayal by the ordinary women who had looked on government as part of the protection – or at least the back-up – that they believed popular culture provided.

In practice these women are becoming increasingly distanced from authority and from a system which constantly seems to be withdrawing from real contact with the public, making people ever less able to access the systems on which the framework of society depends. It is as though the system is trying to hide its multi-faceted face away from public blame, in the hope that everyone will go away and leave it alone. So, after a break-in at your home, it is impossible simply to ring the local police station to get a policeman to visit to assess the crime and discover any clues which might help solve it. Instead the victim is asked to leave a message on an answering machine. Maybe later someone might ring back with a crime number for the insurance company. Maybe, in a mass-media-sponsored dream, but not in the realm of real experience.

As a result, we are seeing a mass public disengagement from government.

17

For many, popular culture as a whole still provides the only possible escape route from a failing system. But now the established mass media which gives voice to popular culture is in trouble. Recession is forcing it to reinvent its own power base. Its traditional mainstays – television, fashion, newspapers and magazines, music as a commodity – are all suffering from disastrously contracting markets.

In response, popular culture is changing tack. In part, it may be cutting itself loose from the way it reflects people's loss of confidence in everything to do with government. Also, it may be responding to a new distrust growing amongst its core market, ordinary women. If so, these women, whose ability to express themselves as popular-culture consumers is hit by the spending crisis, appear to be starting to turn away from the very popular culture which empowered them and gave them political importance. That is calling into question the future of the mass media itself.

Popular culture, however, is already manipulating its own potentially catastrophic decline. If the mass-media boom is over, it must find a new market to expand into. Popular culture in all its aspects has to adapt or die.

So it is moving out of its traditional fields of operation – shops, broadcasting, newspapers, magazines, fashion, advertising and the rest. Or, rather, it is recycling them. The mass-media imperative for growth in demand has now moved it into new electronic technology and the Internet.

That is, into a new form of mass media which operates outside the traditional government which is becoming marginalised in the lives of ever more ordinary people. And government, it seems, is running scared; it has had to make itself available to the public on the Internet, and it is already using its facilities to transmit its own messages.

Popular culture, in fact, has diverted its interests from ordinary women at the terrestrial level to concentrate on all those becoming disassociated from the established system and becoming part of virtual, not real, society. Through the Internet it is providing them – and particularly the young – with a kind of alternative society they can create as a framework for their own lives. It operates a bit like the black market, simply bypassing the complexities of regulation to operate outside the structure of society.

This is not simply a virtual social system, unreal life played out in the ether. It allows everyone with the right electronic device to function in a normal life with friends and shopping and entertainment and financial transactions on screen virtually without reference to the tangible world beyond the computer screen. Scientific research and social surveys can be carried out; educational courses can be accessed to study for qualifications; shopping, interior design, insurance, registration, tax, banking . . . all important social functions now carried out on-line without actual human contact.

Popular culture's present target market is as always the young, the Millennials. It should be noted that here again popular culture has brought about a new gender equality among these young people, but this time it is dominated by women and women's interests, not men and theirs. Now it is commonplace for Millennials to live more fully on the Internet than they do within the social system. That is where they are educated, where they do their revision for exams, where they chat and meet and date and play poker and – one in four of them, it's claimed – download pornography. They bypass parental authority. They can bypass strictly regulated arms of government, too, like the education system, or even the NHS.

The Millennials have no respect for anyone who claims authority over them. In true popular-culture style, they have no interest in what those outside their own group do or say. They are only motivated by an assumption of entitlement to whatever they want. They see this as an automatic right bestowed on them by virtue of being young and 'deserving'. Society endorses their sense of entitlement not out of respect but out of fear that they are out of control. They seem to operate largely outside the physical controls of all social authorities.

Also, of course, society needs their spending potential. That potential is not limited to what the young will spend on themselves, but also includes the money that will be spent on them.

Their empty arrogance and lack of respect for those outside their peer group are making new demands on popular culture itself. Unable to forge satisfying human relationships in the real world, Millennials retreat into alliances carried on via the web on Facebook or MySpace where they can be accepted at their own valuation.

The Millennials' disassociation from 'real' society raises disturbing questions for popular culture. Where there was once an overlap between age groups in which they shared elements of cultural experience, this common ground has dwindled almost to nothing.

The Millennials tend not to watch the same mass-market

television as their predecessors. Advertisers as always want to target the young as the new growth potential in the market, but as all forms of visual popular culture show a decline in audience figures, and a marked fall-off in their appeal to the young, the ad-men look elsewhere. Independent television is struggling to survive this disaffection. Newspapers and magazines, which have been trying to target a younger readership without much success, are now seeing their profitability slashed as advertisers desert the printed page to target youth on the web. Older readers are left in no doubt that they are being marginalised. As sales of national newspapers plummet, these are moving into publishing on-line. They are 'read' on personal electronic gadgets via the Internet, and the conventional printed version of the paper often refers readers directly to the website for more information. There they can see videos, or full, unedited versions of interviews which appeared edited in the paper.

Music has never been more popular, but no one is buying it; they listen instead on iPods, go to live concerts, and buy the T-shirts. The Sony Reader provides electronic books on screen, 160 books stored on a portable gadget the size of a single paperback.

The commercial interest in popular culture has changed. Until the last decade, consumer demand was created through the images popular culture created via its various media incarnations which first showed women what was desirable and possible, then guided them towards self-expression and becoming the image, living the dream. Now popular culture's market is for the technology which creates an illusion of participating in a common dream.

Where once the demarcation between dream and reality

involved a physical connection to the real world – being in a shop, putting on a record or tape, turning on the TV – there was always a reality check. Now that is changing because people carry about their persons the technology to access the dream as an extension of themselves; the head-phones which bring them music are in their own ears; they hold television programmes or a book or the day's news in the palm of their hands. It is much easier for them to lose touch not just with reality, but with the physical outside world. It's easy to see that they can get the impression that they *are* the world.

And, indeed, via new technological advances popular culture now makes it possible for them to be the focus of their own world. And they don't need to earn enough in 'outside' society to do it. Once the technology is bought, most of this cultural content is free.

But where does this leave the ordinary women who, all their lives, many of them, have looked to popular culture to define and express themselves? Disenchanted with government, which embraced popular culture and then failed them, and no longer fulfilled by the mass media which has lost interest in them, there is little left for them to hang on to of the popular culture which first empowered them but is now in terminal decline.

These women, too, have followed the vestiges of their old dreams to the computer in the hope of resurrecting them.

The Internet now makes it possible for millions of ordinary women of the Me Generation – the mothers of the Millennials – to join their alienated children in creating the world in their own image. We have already seen the way that intense personal relationships forged and pursued on-line between fictional personae have blurred reality. This also applies to professional relationships – the web offers legal, medical, financial, all sorts of advice and consultation to apply to their 'real' lives.

It also provides popular culture with new marketing directions. The Bebo social networking site, for example, can use the information its 10.7 million users provide about themselves to tailor the advertising included on these users' personal access points to them individually. It seems the mass media has reached a point where it does not need the mass; it creates an individual persona for the user aimed specifically at their interests, their preferences, and their activities. Now, technically, two generations whose real worlds are bounded by concentration on Me can actually create a sublimated alternative society online where they create and run their own world without regard to the rest of society.

Millions of us already operate to some extent in a virtual parallel society like this, while beyond the dreamworld 'real' government and the social institutions carry on as though nothing has changed. For older people particularly, there are still habitual connections to this traditional social structure, but, as more of us increasingly disengage from institutions and authorities we perceive as having failed us, this traditional system is under threat.

The constituency of this virtual parallel society is a substantial one. A survey quoted in the *Independent* newspaper in January 2008 claimed that efforts were being made to ban online social networking at work because UK office workers spend £130 million worth of company time each day browsing online.

In a way it is as revolutionary as what happened to that

first generation of women empowered by popular culture, the ordinary women who lived quite different lives in their heads from the reality of the everyday domestic round of their traditional role in family life.

But of course it's not the same because it's hard to see how the two worlds can co-exist in future. The virtual world lacks the social layers and the political dimensions of the real world. It is created in the intellectual vacuum which is popular culture, where there is no morality, a distorted view of justice, and no social responsibility. There have been breakdowns of governmental systems before – in Germany before Hitler, and in Russia before the Bolsheviks.

George Orwell, writing in 1940, raises the question of totalitarianism in Britain in his essay *England Your England.* He believed that the British were constitutionally unlikely to entertain such a concept.

But what's happening here and now is different because it is happening this time in a female-orientated society, where power has been vested in the mass of women who have acquired it incidentally, not deliberately. Because of the nature of their empowerment, through a popular culture which has channelled them towards greed and simplistic emotional reactions, and away from the tested bastions of a social system – experience, responsibility, and some kind of social and political morality – it is questionable whether they can acquire the capacity to take on the real world and operate successfully within it without some kind of external power group behind them.

Women are calling the tune. We have seen all along that ordinary women have never wholly escaped from some sort of need to feel that they are supported, that they are part of some sort of community within which they can look to a kind of father figure who will protect and guide them. That father figure might once have been husband, or male friends, or an adviser, or popular culture as a shared source of empowerment, or, yes, government and the state. In Britain today, women have found all these wanting. Now the crucial question is where such women might look next for their new protector and leader.

Orwell describes the totalitarian idea as a society where there is no such thing as law, there is only power. In the light of years of reactive government which has consistently degraded the rule of law, there is a bleak prospect that women who uncritically tolerated bad laws as a means of feeling safe in a mass-media-made society might look instead to a person or system prepared to take and use power without bothering them with the effort of making their own rational decisions.

This is a question that particularly applies to Britain. In other countries, the demarcation between reality and adherence to the brain-sapping images of popular culture is not so starkly drawn. This is partly because in the UK over-dependence on the welfare state has corroded self-reliance and respect for individual responsibility. It is also partly because throughout the rest of Europe women have not become so dependent on popular culture. For example, 40 per cent of British adults with Internet access use networking sites; in Italy the figure is 22 per cent, in France 17 per cent.

But the difference for the British also involves the profile of ordinary women here, and the comparative scarcity of change-agents amongst them. When Dr Christine de Panafieu spoke to the Royal Society of Arts about her research into the sort of women needed to bring about social change, she called British women 'the laggards of Europe'. The British women in her audience were outraged. But their indignant reaction was not to discuss the truth and significance of her findings; they did not try to prove her wrong. They simply tried to cast doubt on her research methods, and question whether, given that her findings were true, they should be made public. They accused her of not knowing what she was talking about because British women were 'a special case'.

But why were those women so insistent that they were 'a special case'? Do British women see themselves as in some way handicapped; or, because they were made powerful by the superficial unrealities of popular culture, somehow entitled to special treatment as inadequate to deal with real life?

If only women would see the source of their empowerment in that light, there might be some prospect that they could, one day, engage with reality without reference to the emotional, irrational representations of popular culture.

However, the sort of reversion to victimhood on display at the Royal Society of Arts that day is the classic reaction of the women empowered by popular culture when faced with grim facts rather than a comforting dreamworld.

And what is popular culture's response to that? There's bound to be an Internet website you can ask for an answer.

Or, perhaps, it's time to start thinking.